The Complete
Shabbat Synagogue
Companion

THE COMPLETE SHABBAT SYNAGOGUE COMPANION

FIRST EDITION
Copyright ©2000
The Jewish Learning Group, Inc.

the
JEWISH
LEARNING GROUP

1-(888)-56-LEARN
www.JewishLearningGroup.com

ISBN 1-891293-12-5

Acknowledgements

A special thanks to Rabbi-Dr. Nissan Mindel O.B.M., past Editor-in-Chief of the Kehot Publication Society, for permitting me to include portions of his book, *My Prayer*.

To Rabbis Eli Cohen, Aaron Goldstein, Pinny Herman, Mendel Herson, Chaim Mentz, and to countless other lay-leaders, for their advice, proof reading, and encouragement.

To Rabbi Sholom Ber Chaikin, for giving so selflessly of his valuable time to read, amend, and refine the material presented here.

A special thanks to Sarah Talalay for proofing the manuscript, and to everyone else who helped make this book a possibility and a reality.

To accurately represent the Hebrew vowels we have devised the following system, which will enable you to pronounce the Hebrew words more accurately:

Hebrew:	Transliteration:	Example:
כ or ח	ch	Challah
ָ	ö	Law
ַ	a	Hurrah
ֵ	ay	Today
ֶ	e	Leg
ְ	'	Avid
ֹ or וֹ	o	Tone
ִ	i	Key
ֻ or וּ	u	Lunar
ַי	ai	Aisle
ָי	oy	Toy

Table of Contents

A Quick Prayer Primer	7
A Quick Shabbat Primer	26
Prayer for Welcoming the Shabbat	40
The Friday Evening Services	50
The Shabbat Morning Services	69
Inspirational Stories	146
Quick How-To Guides	154
Synagogue Glossary	157

-A Quick Prayer Primer-

Odd Man Out

It may be your first time in a synagogue, or the hundredth, but the feeling may be the same. You say to yourself, 'I like it here, it feels good and I know I am doing the right thing, but I don't feel as if I am *really* participating, I don't feel that I really *connect.*'

You may find comfort in the following fact: An average 35 year old observant Jew has prayed over 36,000 (!) services (three times a day on average). No wonder it appears to be so easy for him or her. Imagine how the Speaker of the House feels on his first day on his job in the Congress and how comfortable he becomes at the end of his term. He memorized the protocol, he feels "at home."

So don't beat yourself up so much if on your tenth, or even hundredth, time to the synagogue you feel like a young child in Einstein's lab. This is normal, and most importantly, reading this book will help you learn exactly what you can do about it.

Let's Talk Some Shop

From our school years we can remember our parents and teachers telling us that proper preparation saves lots of perspiration. And as much as we hated to hear it, they were right. So, to make our parents proud, we'll start at the beginning, and really become prepared for our next visit to the synagogue.

Let's start by defining prayer. Prayer is a big word, it carries a lot of "baggage." One person may conjure up an image of a servant and his master; another may think of prayer as something you do only when in trouble; a student might think back to the day of his college finals. But, what do we, as Jews, believe and know about prayer?

God: Pray to me

Prayer is a commandment of God. We are told to pray to Him for our needs, and in our prayers we often address God as our Merciful Father, or as our Father in Heaven, for God regards us, and we regard ourselves, as His children.

You may ask, Why do we have to pray to God for our needs? Doesn't God know our needs even better than we do ourselves? Is not God, by His very nature, good and kind, and always willing to do us good? After all, children do not "pray" to their parents to feed them, and clothe them, and protect them; why should we pray to our Heavenly Father for such things?

The answer to these questions is not hard to find after a little reflection. It has been amply explained by our wise Sages, including the great teacher and guide, Maimonides. He lived some 800 years ago, and was one of the greatest codifiers of Jewish law. He wrote the following concerning prayer:

"We are told to offer up prayers to God, in order to establish firmly the true principle that God takes notice of our ways, that He can make them successful if we serve Him, or disastrous if we disobey Him; that success and failure are not the result of chance or accident." As is the case with all other commandments that God has given to the Jewish people, the commandment to pray is not for His sake but for ours.

And you are right, God does not need our prayers; He can do without our prayers, but *we* cannot do without our prayers. It is good for *us* to acknowledge *our* dependence on God for our very life, our health, our daily bread, and our general welfare.

We do so every day, and many times a day. We need to remind ourselves that our life and happiness are a gift from our Creator, and in turn we try to be worthy of God's kindnesses and favors to us.

God does not owe us anything; yet He gives us everything. We should try to do the same for our fellow men and grant favors freely. We should express our gratitude to God not merely in words, but in deeds: By obeying His commands and living our daily life the way God wants us to – especially because it is all for our own good.

Knowing that God is good and that nothing is impossible for Him to do, we can go about our life with a deep sense of confidence and security. Even in times of distress we will not despair, knowing that in some way (best known to God) whatever happens to us is for our own good. It is a blessing in disguise.

Nevertheless, we pray to God to help us out of our distress, and grant us the good that is not hidden or disguised. That He give us the good that is obvious even to humans who have limited understanding.

We gain strength, courage and hope by trusting in God, and our daily prayers strengthen this trust in God. "In God We Trust" has been our Jewish motto since we first became a people.

Let's go a bit deeper

The Hebrew word תפלה (*tefillah*) is generally translated as "prayer," but this is not an accurate translation. To pray means to beg, beseech, implore, and the like, and we have a number of Hebrew words that more accurately convey this meaning. Our daily prayers are not merely requests to God to give us our daily needs and nothing more. Of course, such requests are also included in our prayers, but mostly our prayers are much more than that, as we shall see.

Going Up

Our Sages declare that the ladder which our forefather Jacob saw in his dream, with angels of God "going up and coming down," was also the symbol of prayer. By showing the ladder to Jacob in his dream, a ladder which "stood on the earth and reached into the heaven," our Sages explain, God showed Jacob that prayer is like a ladder which connects the earth with the heaven, man with God.

The meaningful words of prayer, the good resolutions which it brings forth, are transformed into angels that go to God, Who then sends them down with blessings in return. That is why Jacob saw in his dream that angels were "going up and coming down," although one would have expected angels to first come down and *then* go up.

Thus, what we said about prayer in answer to the question: "Why do we pray?" is but the first step on the "ladder" of prayer. Prayer also has to do with things that are on a higher level than daily material needs – namely spiritual things.

A Time of Self-Judgment

The Hebrew word תפלה (*tefillah*) comes from the verb פלל (*pallel*), "to judge." The reflexive verb להתפלל (*lehitpallel*) "to pray" also means, "to judge oneself." Thus, the time of prayer is a time of self-judgment and self-evaluation.

When a person addresses himself to God and prays for His blessings, he must inevitably search his heart and examine whether he measures up to the standards of daily conduct which God has prescribed for man to follow. If he is honest with himself, he will be filled with humility, realizing that he hardly merits the blessings and favors for which he is asking. This is why we stress in our prayers God's infinite goodness and mercies. We pray to God to grant us our heart's desires, not because we merit them, but even though we may not deserve them.

This is also why our prayers, on weekdays, contain a confession of sins which we may have committed, knowingly or unknowingly. We pray for God's forgiveness, and resolve to better ourselves.

So we see how prayer can also help us lead a better life in every respect, by living more fully the way of the Torah and mitzvot, which God commanded us.

Jewish Customer Service

On an even higher level, prayer becomes עבודה *(avodah)*, "service." The Torah commands us "to serve God with our hearts," and our Sages say: "What kind of service is 'service of the heart?' — it is prayer." In this sense, prayer is meant to purify our hearts and our nature.

The plain Hebrew meaning of *avodah* is "work." We work with a raw material and convert it into a refined and finished product. In the process, we remove the impurities, or roughness, of the raw material, whether it is a piece of wood or a rough diamond, and make it into a thing of usefulness or beauty.

The tanner, for example, takes raw hide and converts it into fine leather. The parchment on which a Torah Scroll, a *Mezuzah*, or *Tefillin* is written, is made of the hide of a kosher animal. Raw wool full of grease and other impurities, through stages of "work," is made into a fine wool, from which we can make not only fine clothes, but also a *Tallit* (prayer shawl), or *Tzitzit* (fringed garment).

Diamonds are Forever

The Jewish people have been likened in the Torah to soil and earth, and have been called God's "land of desire." The saintly Ba'al Shem Tov, the founder of Chassidism, explained it this way: The earth is full of treasures, but they are often buried deep inside. It is necessary to dig for them; and when you discover them, you still have to clear away the impurities, refine them or polish them, as in the case of gold or diamonds.

Similarly, every Jew is full of wonderful treasures of character — modesty, kindness and other natural traits — but sometimes they are buried deep and covered up by "soil" and "dust," which have to be cleared away.

Define Refined

We speak of a person of good character as a "refined" person, or of "refined" character. It is often difficult, to overcome such bad traits as pride, anger, jealousy, which may be quite "natural" but are still unbecoming for a human being, especially a Jew.

Tefillah, in the sense of *avodah*, is the "refinery" where the impurities of character are done away with. These bad character traits stem from the "animal" soul in man, and are "natural" to it. But we are endowed with a "Divine" soul, which is a spark of Godliness itself, and the treasure of all the wonderful qualities which make a man superior to an animal.

13

During proper prayer, our Divine soul speaks to God, and even the animal soul is filled with holiness. We realize that we stand before the Holy One, blessed be He, and the whole material world with all its pains and pleasures seems to melt away. We become aware of things that really matter and are truly important; even as we pray for life, health and sustenance, we think of these things in their deeper sense: a life that is worthy to be called "living"; health that is not only physical, but above all spiritual; sustenance – the things that truly sustain us in this world and in the world to come – the Torah and mitzvot.

We feel cleansed and purified by such "service," and when we return to our daily routine, the feeling of purity and holiness lingers and raises our daily conduct to a level fitting for a member of the people called a "kingdom of priests and a holy nation."

Attached to God

The highest level on the "ladder" of prayer is reached when we are so inspired as to want nothing but the feeling of attachment with God. On this level *tefillah* is related to the verb (used in Mishnaic Hebrew) **תופל** (*tofel*), to "attach," "join," or "bind together," as two pieces of a broken vessel are pieced together to make it whole again.

Our soul is truly a part of God, and therefore longs to be reunited with, and reabsorbed in, Godliness, just as a small flame when it is put close to a larger flame, is absorbed into the larger flame. We may not be aware of this longing, but it is there nonetheless.

Our soul has, in fact, been called the "candle of God." The flame of a candle is restless, striving upwards, to break away, as it were, from the wick and body of the candle; for such is the nature of fire — to strive upwards. Our soul, too, strives upwards, like that flame. This is also one of the reasons why a Jew naturally sways while praying. For prayer is the means whereby we attach ourselves to God, with a soulful attachment of "spirit to spirit," and in doing so our soul flutters and soars upward, to be united with God.

Mitzvah Bar

Let us examine this idea more closely. Every mitzvah which God has commanded us to do, and which we perform as a sacred commandment, attaches us to God. The word mitzvah is related to the Aramaic word צוותא (*tzavta*), "togetherness," or "company." In English, too, we have the verb "to enjoin," which means "to command," for the commandment is the bond that joins together the person commanded with the person commanding, no matter how far apart they may be in distance, rank or position.

When a king commands a humble servant to do something, this establishes a bond between the two. The humble servant feels greatly honored that the king has taken notice of him and has given him something to do, and that he, an insignificant person, can do something to please the great king. It makes him eager to be worthy of the king's attention and favor.

If this is so in the case of every mitzvah, it is even more so in the case of prayer. For nothing brings us closer to God than prayer, when it is truly the outpouring of the soul and, therefore, makes for an "attachment of spirit to spirit," as mentioned earlier. If any mitzvah brings us closer to God, prayer (on the level we are speaking) is like being embraced by God. There is no greater pleasure or fulfillment than the wonderful spiritual uplift and blissfulness resulting from prayer.

Prose that Rose

Prayer, we said, is like a "ladder" of many rungs. To get to the top of it, we must start at the bottom and steadily rise upwards. To enable us to do so, our prayers have been composed prophetically by our saintly Prophets and Sages of old, and have been ordered also like a "ladder," steadily leading us to greater and greater inspiration. We must, therefore, become familiar with our prayers: first of all their plain meaning, then their deeper meaning, and finally the whole "order" of the service.

The Three Daily Prayers

Jewish Law requires us to pray three times daily: Morning, afternoon and evening. These prayers are called *Shacharit* (morning prayer), *Minchah* (afternoon prayer) and *Arvit*, or *Maariv* (evening prayer).

Our Sages tell us that our Patriarchs, Abraham, Isaac and Jacob originally introduced the custom of praying three times a day.

Abraham introduced prayer in the morning; Isaac instituted afternoon prayer, and Jacob added one at night.

In the *Zohar* (or *kabbalah*; the mystical part of the Torah) it is explained further that each of the three Patriarchs represented a particular quality which they introduced into the service of God. Abraham served God with love; Isaac with awe; and Jacob with mercy. Not that each lacked the qualities of the others, but each had a particular quality that was more prominent.

Thus Abraham distinguished himself especially in the quality of kindness (חסד) and love (אהבה), while Isaac excelled especially in the quality of strict justice (דין) and reverence (יראה), while Jacob inherited both these qualities, bringing out a new quality which combined the first two into the well-balanced and lasting quality of truth (אמת) and mercy (רחמים).

We, the children of Abraham, Isaac and Jacob, have inherited all three great qualities of our Patriarchs, enabling us to serve God and pray to Him with love and fear (awe) and mercy. The quality of mercy comes in when we realize that our soul is a part of Godliness, and we feel pity for it because it is so often distracted from God by the material aspects of daily life.

Life's Big Instruction Book

When the Torah was given to us at Mount Sinai, our way of life was set out for us by God. Torah means "teaching," "instruction," "guidance"; for the Torah teaches us our way of living, including every detail of our daily life.

The Torah contains 613 commandments. Among them is the command to "serve God with all our heart and all our soul." By praying to Him we fulfill not only the commandment of prayer, but also other commandments, such as to love God and to fear Him.

During the first one thousand years or so from the time of Moshe *Rabbeinu* (Moses), there was no set order of prayer. Each individual was duty-bound to pray to God every day, but the form of prayer was left to the individual.

There was, however, a set order of service in the *Beit Hamikdash* (the Holy Temple that stood in Jerusalem) in connection with the daily sacrifices, morning and afternoon, with the latter sacrifice extending into the night. On special days, such as Shabbat, Rosh Chodesh (start of a new month) and Festivals, there were also "additional" (*musaf*) sacrifices.

Accordingly, it was not unusual for some Jews to pray three times a day – morning, afternoon, and evening – in their own way. King David, for example, declared that he prayed three times daily, and Daniel (in Babylon) prayed three times daily facing the direction of Jerusalem. There is evidence that, even during the time of the first *Beit Hamikdash*, there were public places of prayer, called *Beit Ha-am*, which the Chaldeans (Babylonians) destroyed, along with the *Beit Hamikdash* and the rest of Jerusalem.

Prayer for Dummies

After the *Beit Hamikdash* was destroyed and the Jews were led into captivity in Babylon, Jews continued to gather and pray in congregation. The places of prayer became like "small sanctuaries." But during the years of exile, the children that were born and raised in Babylon lacked adequate knowledge of the Holy Tongue, Hebrew, and spoke a mixed language.

Therefore, when the Jews returned to their homeland after the seventy years of exile were over, Ezra the Scribe together with the Men of the Great Assembly (consisting of Prophets and Sages, 120 members in all) set the text of the daily prayer, *Shemoneh Esrei* – the "Eighteen Benedictions", and made it a permanent institution and duty in Jewish life to recite this prayer three times daily. Ever since then it became part of Jewish Law (*halacha*) for each and every Jew to pray this ordained and fixed order of prayer three times daily, corresponding to the daily sacrifices in the *Beit Hamikdash*, with additional (*Musaf*) prayers on Shabbat, Rosh Chodesh and Festivals, and a special "closing" prayer (*Neilah*) on Yom Kippur.

Thus, the main parts of the daily prayers were formulated by our Sages, which still are the main parts of our morning and evening prayers.

The *Shema* was included in the morning and evening prayers, and the daily Psalm which used to be sung by the Levites in the *Beit Hamikdash*, became part of the morning prayer. Other Psalms of

David were included in the morning prayer, and special benedictions before and after the *Shema* were added. By the time the Mishna was recorded by Rabbi Judah the Prince about the year 3,910 (some 500 years after Ezra; 150 C.E.), and especially by the time the Talmud was completed (some 300 years later, or about 1500 years ago), the basic order of our prayers, as we know them now, had been formulated.

The Recipe

The morning service consists of the following sections: 1) The blessings upon rising from bed, 2) The chapters of praise, 3) The blessings for the *Shema*, 4) The *Shema*, 5) The *Amidah*, and 6) The concluding prayers.

1) Upon waking in the morning we express our gratitude to God for the rest we had, for giving us back all our senses and restoring strength to our weary limbs. We thank God also for the great privilege of being a Jew and serving God, for having given us His holy Torah, and so on.

2) Then we recite Psalms of praise to God, describing His majesty and might, as the Creator of Heaven and Earth and all creatures, His loving-kindness and goodness in taking care of all creatures.

3-4) Having thus been inspired by God's goodness and love, we declare the Unity of God, and we take upon ourselves to love God and observe all His commands.

5) After all the above, we come to the main part of the prayer — the *Amidah*, in which we put our requests before God.

6) We then conclude the service with appropriate Psalms and prayers.

This is again one of the reasons why prayer has been likened to a ladder ("Jacob's Ladder") connecting earth and heaven. For the sections of our prayer indeed are like the rungs of a ladder, one leading to the other.

Shmoozing with God

So, as we see from the above, prayer time in the synagogue is too valuable to blow on shmooz, news, and maybe even a little snooze. It is a sacred time of real communion with God, a time of self-analysis and self-growth.

Think of it as being invited to participate in an intricate experiment in a laboratory, or given a chance to take part in exciting activities on the trading floor of the Stock Exchange, or for that matter, an opportunity to change things in your own life, and instead we sit there lounging with a newspaper or making small talk, all while this great stuff is happening all around us.

So, we are indeed ready to give 60 or 90 minutes of our attention to the matter at hand in the synagogue and leave the socializing for the golf course, or Sundays, or the Kiddush that usually follows the services on Shabbat.

But you may ask, what do we do then with all this "new" free time? And how do I "turn on" this mystic connection with God?

Enter the Prayer Book

For many years during the period of the Holy Temple (some 2,000 years ago), the Jewish people prayed by heart. As times changed, and younger generations were not learning the prayers, it was time to set them in fixed order in a book. This book was called a *Siddur*. The Siddur became our traditional prayer book, containing the three daily prayers; the prayers for Shabbat, Rosh Chodesh and the Festivals.

"Siddur" means "order," since in the Siddur we find our prayers in their proper and fixed order. Sometimes, for the sake of convenience, the Shabbat and Rosh Chodesh prayers may be printed in a separate volume. The prayers for Rosh Hashanah and Yom Kippur are usually printed in separate volumes, called *Machzor* ("cycle"). Sometimes the prayers for the Three Festivals — Pesach, Shavuot and Sukkot — are also printed in separate volumes.

The oldest Siddur that we know of is the Siddur of Rav *Amram Gaon*, Head of the Yeshiva of Sura, in Babylon, about 1,100 years ago. He had prepared it at the request of the Jews of Barcelona, Spain. It contains the arrangements of the prayers for the entire year, including also some laws concerning prayer and customs. It was copied and used the Jews of France and Germany, and was in fact the standard prayer book for all Jewish communities.

Seder Rav Amram Gaon remained in handwritten form for about 1,000 years, until it was printed for the first time in Warsaw in 1865. Rav *Saadia Gaon*, who was head of the Sura Yeshiva less than 100 years after Rav Amram Gaon, arranged a Siddur for the Jews in Arab countries, with explanations and instructions in Arabic. The *Rambam*, Maimonides, in his famous Code of Jewish Law, also prepared the order of the prayers for the whole year (including the Haggadah of Pesach), and included it in his work, following the section dealing with the laws of prayer.

The structure of the prayers remains basically the same. The morning prayers begin with the morning blessings, continue with *Pesukei D'zimra* (Psalms and sections from the Prophets, introduced and concluded by benedictions), followed by the *Shema* (which is also introduced and concluded by a benediction), and continues with the main prayer, *Shemoneh Esrei*, which means "eighteen," because originally this prayer had eighteen blessings (weekday version), and is also known as the *Amidah* ("standing"), because it must be recited in a standing position.

101 ways to Tell God I Love You

So, the Siddur is our "code book," with all the necesary words proven to kindle within us the whole gamut of feelings we need to feel. And the early rabbis did us the greatest favor by putting it all in order.

Suppose you were at a high school reunion, and were suddenly asked to stand up and make a speech about your memories, feelings, perhaps some wishes you had, all in front of a familiar but now estranged crowd. Wouldn't it be easier if you had some outline to get you started?

This is the value of the prayers, their outline, order and sequence, down to the words and letters chosen. They help us experience the befitting emotion.

I know we may not all be poets, but it is really difficult to read through the prayers and *not* feel moved at some point or another to the appropriate feelings. At one time it will be one prayer that does it. Another time a different one. But the goal is always the same.

Feel God, thank God, appreciate what we've got, and ask God to give us strength to pull through for Him, for ourselves, and for the entire Jewish people.

Blast the Rote to Heaven

It is easy, after a while, to read familiar prayers too quickly, or without real concentration. It can become a habit. Yet familiarity need not necessarily make it so, for as we know, people eat three times a day, and usually enjoy every meal. So when we pray and give our prayer a little thought, we can find great inspiration and uplift in them. At least, on the day of Shabbat and Festivals, when we have less to worry about, we can pray with even greater devotion.

The first thing that is essential is at least to know the meaning and translation of the words of the prayers. If we cannot concentrate every day on the entire prayers, it would be a good idea one day to concentrate on one part, the next day on the next part, so that in the course of a week we will have concentrated on all the prayers. Or to make Shabbat the special day on which to work through the prayers like a real mystic.

To get you started, we have provided brief explanations for every single prayer for Friday evening and Shabbat morning services. We have also included English transliterations of key prayers, to assist those to whom the Hebrew language is not yet familiar to read or sing along in the original Hebrew.

It is recommended that you keep this book with you during the services and refer to it for 30 seconds or so before saying each prayer. It will boost the octane of your experience.

Please note: Since one of the prohibited actions on the Shabbat is carrying items from a private domain into a public one, and vice versa, make sure to bring this book to the synagogue before the onset of Shabbat. Alternatively, you can use it before the Shabbat as a study guide in its own right.

-A Quick Shabbat Primer-

Is it a Weak-End or a Strong-Beginning?

Shabbat is not just the seventh day of the week, or the day on which God rested from creating the world. It is much more than that. Shabbat was made by God as a day onto itself, it has its own identity. It is not just a day meant to be absent of work, but now unencumbered by our daily distractions, the day of Shabbat is to be used to connect with our spiritual source.

We also utilize the Shabbat day to stop and appreciate God's creation, and spend time calibrating our 'spiritual compass' for the coming week.

For the 26 hours of Shabbat we cease interacting with the material world. We stop working and creating, all in order to pause and acknowledge the real Creator, lest we become too self-absorbed in our daily grind to remember that all our fortune comes from God, and our work is only a vessel to receive His bountiful blessings.

On Shabbat we remember our main goal and purpose in this world. We are not here only to achieve fame, accumulate riches, or advance technology, but also to refine this material world. This is accomplished by following and living by the ways of the Torah, given to us by God at Mount Sinai.

What better way to spend this holy day than with family and friends, immersing ourselves in prayer and Torah study, and maximizing this golden opportunity which comes to us only once a week.

There are many laws and guidelines that one needs to know to properly observe and extract the best out of the Shabbat. Many books have been written and most are available in Jewish bookstores. They can help you learn more about the Shabbat and assist you as you embark on this wonderful spiritual journey, one which our parents and grand-parents have enjoyed, reaching back more than 3,300 years. Shabbat is a day on which we stand proudly as Jews, proud to be God's light onto the nations, proud to be the bearer of God's way of life.

To obtain a deeper insight into the special nature of this day, what the Shabbat means to us, and what is its universal message, we will dwell briefly on the main aspects of the Shabbat, particularly those that are reflected in Shabbat prayers.

The Shabbat Bride

The Torah tells us that God created the world in six days, and that by the end of the sixth day the heaven and earth and all their hosts were completed. Then God rested from all creative activity, "and God blessed the seventh day and made it holy." Thus, right from the beginning of Creation, God has set the Shabbat day apart from the other days of the week, as a holy day.

But for whom was the Shabbat meant? Who was to accept it, appreciate it, and keep it holy? The answer is found in the following meaningful *Midrash*:

"Rabbi *Shimon ben Yochai* taught: When God created the holy Shabbat, it said to the Holy One, blessed be He: "Every day You created has a mate. Am I to be the only odd one, without a mate?" Replied God, "The Jewish people will be your mate." And so, while the Jewish people stood at the foot of Mount Sinai to receive the Torah and become a nation, God declared (in the Ten Commandments): "Remember the Shabbat day, to keep it holy!" As if to say, "Remember My promise to the Shabbat that the Jewish nation shall be its mate."

The book of *kabbalah* referres to the Jewish people and the Shabbat in terms of bridegroom and bride, and this is why in the Shabbat prayers, the Shabbat is welcomed with the words, *Bo-i chalöh, Bo-i chalöh* — "Welcome, bride; welcome, bride!" The repetition, *Bo-i chalöh,* alludes to the two great qualities of the "bride," being both "blessed" and "holy," as it is written, "And God blessed the seventh day and made it holy." Indeed, according to Rabbi *Yitzchak Arama* in his *Akedat Yitzchak*, the word *L'kadsho* — "to keep it holy" — may be rendered "to betroth it," in the sense of *kiddushin*, marriage.

In this way, our Sages tell us that the Shabbat is uniquely Jewish, that is to say, that the Jewish people and the Shabbat are inseparable; they were destined for each other from the moment of their "birth."

Without the Shabbat the Jewish people is simply unthinkable, just as without the Torah the Jewish people is unthinkable. This is one of the reasons why the Shabbat was equated with all the mitzvot.

Shabbat of Creation

The origin of the Shabbat, referred to as the Shabbat of Creation, is given in the section of *Vayechulu* in the bible (see, Genesis), which is also recited during Shabbat services. Shabbat is not mentioned again explicitly in the Torah until after the story of the Exodus, in connection with the manna.

This heavenly bread did not come down on the Shabbat but, instead, the children of Israel received a double portion on Friday for Shabbat as well. Then Moses told the children of Israel: "See, God has given you this Shabbat."

The Shabbat was nothing new for the children of Israel, for, as our Sages tell us, they had known about it traditionally from the time of Abraham and, indeed, observed it even in Egypt. But on this occasion they received the first laws about Shabbat, and several weeks later they received formal instructions on Shabbat in the Ten Commandments at Mount Sinai.

After the Torah was given to our people, the commandment to observe the Shabbat is repeated in the Torah many times with great emphasis. One of the better known passages about the Shabbat is included in the Shabbat morning prayers:

"And the children of Israel shall keep the Shabbat...as an everlasting covenant. It is a sign between Me and the children of Israel forever: That in six days God made heaven and earth, and on the seventh day He ceased from work and rested."

Here the Torah tells us of the basic significance of the Shabbat as the living sign of God's creation. By keeping the Shabbat, we, the Jewish people, proclaim aloud that God is the Creator of heaven and earth, and we reaffirm the everlasting covenant between God and the Jewish people. God has crowned His creation with the Shabbat, and has given this crown to us. Our Sages of the Talmud expressed it this way: "A precious gift —says God— have I in My treasure stores; its name is Shabbat, and I have given it to you."

Wearing this crown is, of course, a great privilege. But it also places upon us great responsibilities. These are summed up by *Rambam* (Maimonides) as follows:

"The Shabbat is the everlasting sign between God and the people of Israel...He who observes the Shabbat properly, honoring it and delighting in it to the best of his ability, is given a reward in this world, over and above the reward that is reserved for him in the World to Come."

You're Not Working?

More than anything else, it has been the Shabbat that has distinguished the Jewish people from all other nations of the world throughout the ages. For this was not just a matter of a single precept, or custom, but something that is fundamental to the Jewish religion and Jewish way of life.

An entire day of the week (actually 26 hours) is set apart, during which the Jew not only desists from work, closes down stores, factories, workshops and halts all work at home — but is completely transformed into a person of holiness, devoting the time to prayer and study. Even externally this transformation is in evidence — in one's dress, eating, walking and talking.

For thousands of years the nations of the world could not understand this Jewish Shabbat. They, who had not known a rest day in the week altogether, thought it deplorable for an entire nation to take off work for a whole day in the week.

When Haman complained to King Ahasuerus about the "one people, scattered and dispersed among the nations, whose laws are different from those of any other nation," it was Shabbat and the Festivals that he held up to ridicule. Ancient Roman historians called the Jewish people "lazy" and "uncivilized" for their adherence to the Shabbat.

When the nations of the world finally recognized the Torah as a holy book, and called it "The Book" (Bible), they adopted some of its principles. They also introduced a "Sabbath" or "day of rest" into their religions. But it is significant that they made it on Sunday (in Christianity), or on Friday (in Islam). The Shabbat remained Jewish for Jews alone. Although imitation may be the highest form of flattery, nothing in the imitations can approach the original, Divinely ordained, Shabbat, as anyone familiar with the laws of Shabbat and their significance knows.

Remembrance of the Exodus from Egypt

In the Shabbat sanctification ceremony that we conduct upon arriving home from Friday evening services, known as the Kiddush, we thank God for giving us the Shabbat "as a memorial to the work of Creation" and also "as a remembrance of the Exodus from Egypt." These two basic perceptions of Shabbat are derived from the Ten Commandments, the fourth of which deals with Shabbat.

In the first Decalogue it is stated:

"Remember the Shabbat day...for in six days God made heaven and earth, the sea and all that is in them, and ceased work on the seventh day; wherefore God blessed the Shabbat day and sanctified it."

The text in the second Decalogue reads:

"Observe the Shabbat day to keep it holy...And you shall remember that you were a slave in the land of Egypt, and God your God brought you out of there by a mighty hand and by an outstretched arm; therefore, God your God commanded you to keep the Shabbat day."

Commenting on the different aspects of Shabbat as reflected in the Ten Commandments in Exodus and Deuteronomy respectively, the *Ramban* (Nachmanides) explains that, far from being contradictory, they are supportive and complementary. For as the day of rest attesting to the Creation, Shabbat also brings to mind the time when the Jewish people, being enslaved in Egypt, were not free to rest on that day. They had to work on all seven days of the week. Hence, the Torah emphasizes, "in order that your man-servant and your maid-servant may rest as well as you."

In a deeper sense, the *Ramban* continues, the Exodus from Egypt confirmed and deepened our belief without doubt in God as Creator of the universe.

Until the Exodus from Egypt, the belief in One God came down to the Jewish people from Abraham, Isaac and Jacob, the founders of our Jewish nation, along with the unique covenant that had been established between God and the Patriarchs and their descendants. During the centuries of enslavement, however, belief and tradition were put to severe test.

Many, if not most, of the enslaved Jews must have had some doubts whether there really was a Supreme Being, Creator and Master of the world, or if such a Being had not abandoned the world to its devices, or to the mighty Pharaohs. The Exodus from Egypt, with all its wonders and miracles, demonstrated without any doubt that God was truly the Creator and Master of the world, since He was able at will to suspend and change the laws of nature.

Moreover, the Exodus from Egypt demonstrated, too, that Divine *Hashgachah* ("watchfulness," providence) extends to every particular and detail of the created order, to humans as well as to the lower orders of animal and plant life, even to the inanimate.

A third essential element of the Exodus experience was the revelation of prophecy. It established the fact that the Creator not only bestowed upon Moses the gift of prophecy, but made him the greatest of all Prophets (forty-eight men and seven women, according to our Sages). It was at the miraculous crossing of *Yam Suf* ("Red Sea; Sea of Reeds") that the liberated Israelites attained complete "trust in God and in Moses His servant" — meaning, "in the prophecy of Moses His servant."

This belief in the truth of Moses' prophecy is no less a cornerstone of our Jewish faith than the belief in the two fundamental principles mentioned above: namely, the existence of a Supreme Being as Creator of the world, and Divine Providence extending to the smallest detail of the created order. For, although the entire nation witnessed the Divine Revelation at Mount Sinai and heard the Decalogue, the entire Torah with all its 613 mitzvot was transmitted through Moses.

In light of the above, the *Ramban* points out, we can appreciate the Talmudic declaration that "Shabbat equi-balances all the mitzvot," since by keeping Shabbat we attest to the truth of all the fundamental principles of our faith: Creation *ex nihilo*, Divine Providence and Divine Prophecy.

34

Thus, *Ramban* concludes, Shabbat is a remembrance of the Exodus from Egypt, while the Exodus from Egypt, in turn, is a memorial to Shabbat of Creation.

To Make the Shabbat

Referring to the above-mentioned verse, "And the children of Israel shall "keep" (*v'sham'ru*) the Shabbat, to "make" (*la-asos*) the Shabbat," etc., our Sages declare that to "keep" refers to all the laws pertaining to the cessation of work and all that we may not do on Shabbat; and to "make" refers to all things that we have to put into the Shabbat, to honor it, delight in it and fill it with holiness through prayer and study.

Jews make the Shabbat and Shabbat makes the Jewish people. That is what is meant by referring to the Shabbat and the Jewish people as real mates, as mentioned earlier. Indeed, more than the Jewish people kept the Shabbat, the Shabbat has kept the Jewish people, for more than anything else, the Shabbat unites all Jews, in all parts of the world.

The Shabbat is also a reminder to all mankind that it must persistently move toward the "day that is all Shabbat" — a world where all the nations of the world will recognize the sovereignty of the Creator and His rule on earth, a world in which there is no strife, nor violence, nor injustice, for the spirit of Shabbat (peace) will permeate the whole world.

Preparing for the Shabbat

A richly satisfying Shabbat never just happens, it is the result of an effort made all week long. It is related that one of our great Sages would bring home a special food item he found in the market during the week and say, This is for the Shabbat. When upon finding something of better quality and taste he would replace the earlier item and say, *This* is for the Shabbat. His whole week was permeated with the Shabbat.

Now, Shabbat preparations does not only surround food. There are many other preparations that must be done before the onset of the Shabbat at sundown on Friday. For a fuller understanding of these I refer you to the "Laws of Shabbat" section of the "Code of Jewish Law." There are also many other wonderful books which delve into the laws and inner-workings of the Shabbat, and I recommend everyone seeking to observe an authentic Shabbat to study them. For introductory purposes I will present a few of the major points:

Clothing:

It is mandated in Jewish law that we should wear clean, respectable attire on the day of Shabbat. Today this is usually translated to mean a white shirt and dark pants for men and boys, and a modest dress for woman and girls. Many people even have a special suite or dress worn only for the Shabbat.

Food:

There are three special meals on Shabbat. 1) Friday night after the services, 2) Shabbat morning after the services, and 3) late Shabbat afternoon. The table is usually decked with a white table cloth, and some have the custom to have the Shabbat candles placed in the center of the table (at candle lighting), to enjoy the radiant light of Shabbat during the meal. The finest cutlery and dishwear are also used to further glorify this day.

Among the many traditional foods prepared for the Shabbat, you will find special braided bread called Challa, along with dishes of fish, meat, and tasty wines. This is no random selection. This order of foods was handed down to us by our Sages, and this precept was extracted from the commandment in the Torah, 'to honor the Shabbat with food and drink'.

Appropriate food for the Shabbat is so important that we are taught that one who cannot afford to purchase any of the above food items, must borrow the money to purchase them!

Work:

As you know by now, Shabbat is a day of rest, and as discussed earlier, this rest is not only a "quite time," to rejuvenate our energies as it were. While this may also be the case, the rest on Shabbat means the cessation of any creative function we normally do during the week. This is to enable us to recognize and appreciate the One who really does the creating, our God in Heavens.

This means no beepers, cell-phones, faxes, TV, movies, golf, tennis, shopping, sowing, rowing, swimming, skating, boating, flying, lighting fires, baking bread, barbecuing, etc.

There is a relevant stories I would like to share with you:

A young person came to a Rabbi and asked, "Why are there so many restrictions on the Shabbat? I feel so imprisoned! I can't watch TV, I can't use the phone, I can't turn on lights, I can't go to the mall."

The Rabbi replied: "Did I use the word prohibited?"

"What do you mean, Rabbi?" exclaimed the young man. "You taught us that you can't do this and can't do that, and that is how one guards the sanctity of the Shabbat."

The Rabbi stroked his long beard and said, "Young lad, you got me wrong. What I am saying is that on Shabbat you are permitted *not* to watch TV, *not* to answer the phones, *not* to check for e-mail, *not* to cook, so that you can freely devote the *entire day* to your spirituality. Don't you see how it is more liberating than imprisoning?"

Indeed, how often do we feel we can have the "permission" to close out the world outside and be with ourselves and our family? Most of us can agree that if we were able to "invest" at least one set of 24 hours a week to "tune-out" the world, and "tune-in" to our family and spirituality, we will be rewarded with the rich happiness and fulfillment that Shabbat was meant to provide the Jewish People.

Self:

We spend a portion of Shabbat day in prayer, a portion learning Torah, and a portion connecting with the people that are important to us.

Shabbat is also an opportune time to do "spiritual accounting" for the outgoing week. We focus on how we can better ourselves in areas surrounding our family and work, and make resolutions to change for the better during the week to come.

Family:

No need to mention the benefit of the unity that is fostered when the family spends time together, eating, drinking, and connecting with one another. It is also customary for parents to learn with their children topics of Jewish value during the day of Shabbat.

It is indeed not in vain that the Shabbat was called by family psychologists, "The glue that keeps the family together."

Prayer for Welcoming the Shabbat

The Friday evening services begin here. When a Festival or *Chol HaMoed*, intermediate days of the Festivals, falls on Shabbat, begin with *Mizmor L'dovid*, A Psalm by David.

The order of the service is as follows:

1. Welcoming of the Shabbat

2. The Evening services

3. The *Shema*

4. The Amidah, silent prayer

5. Concluding prayers

We begin the service with six Psalms, each Psalm represents a day of creation. There are three main themes that run through them all:

1. The spirit and joy that permeates these Psalms puts us in the proper mood for welcoming the Shabbat.

2. That the creation of this world is the "crown" of God's work, thus evoking from us our acknowledgement of His majesty and our submission to His will, as is expressed in the Torah.

3. Anticipation of the Messianic era in which our material world will attain the ultimate perfection for which it was destined.

Come, let us sing...   לְכוּ נְרַנְּנָה לַיְיָ...

In this Psalm we find Adam's first words after God breathed into him the Breath of Life: "Come, let us prostrate ourselves and bow down; let us bend the knee before the Lord our Maker." He called to all creatures of the world to acknowledge the Creator and to submit to His will.

The Psalm also notes the special relationship we have with God. How we are His people and He looks after us as a shepherd tends to his flock.

It concludes with the miraculous exodus from Egypt, where God first showed His personal concern for our people.

Sing to the Lord...   שִׁירוּ לַיְיָ ...

This Psalm too begins with a call to sing God's praises. It speaks of the Messianic era, when the extraordinary salvation that God will bring to our people will call for a new kind of praise.

The revelation of God's majesty in those future days will cause all mankind to worship God with a sense of holiness and awe.

🎵 **Transliteration:**

Shiru la-donöy shir chödösh, shiru la-donöy köl hö-öretz. Shiru la-donöy bör'chu sh'mo, bas'ru mi-yom l'yom y'shu-öso. Sap'ru vago-yim k'vodo, b'chöl hö-amim nif-l'osöv. Ki gödol adonöy u-m'hulöl m'od, norö hu al köl elohim. Ki köl elohay hö-amim elilim—va-adonöy shöma-yim ösöh. Hod v'hödör l'fönöv, oz v'sif-eres b'mik-dösho. Hövu la-donöy mish-p'chos amim, hövu la-donöy kövod vö-oz. Hövu la-donöy k'vod sh'mo, s'u minchöh u-vo-u l'chatz'rosöv. Hishtachavu la-donöy b'had'ras kodesh, chilu mipönöv köl hö-öretz. Im'ru vago-yim adonöy mölöch, af tikon tayvayl bal timot, yödin amim b'mayshörim. Yis-m'chu hashöma-yim v'sögayl hö-öretz, yir-am hayöm u-m'lo-o. Ya-aloz södai v'chöl asher bo, öz y'ran'nu köl atzay yö-ar. Lif'nay adonöy ki vö, ki vö lishpot hö-öretz, yishpot tayvayl b'tzedek, v'amim be-emunöso.

When the Lord...   ...יְיָ מָלָךְ

This Psalm continues the theme of Messianic Era. At that time it will be an occasion for tremendous rejoicing, for the world will then enter the era of its fulfillment and perfection.

While God himself will still be hidden from man — as if he were surrounded by a cloud and by darkness — nevertheless, His reign on earth will be clearly recognized by all.

The words 'Light is sown for the righteous' bear significant meaning. The good works that a person does are likend to the sowing or planting of seeds.

The 'light' sown refers to the Torah and commandments. Since the Torah is God's thought and knowledge, it is attached to infinity. Thus when we perform a *mitzvah*, commandment, though the event may be transient, the effects are enduring, and benefit us forever.

A Psalm. Sing...   מִזְמוֹר שִׁירוּ...

This Psalm speaks of the Messianic era. King David acclaims God's wondrous acts when the time will come to reveal His might and glory.

During the long and dark exile the nations of the world mocked and derided the Jewish people, saying that God has forgotten and forsaken them, and they could be persecuted without fear of punishment. But those wicked nations are due to find out how wrong they were, as we note here in this Psalm.

When the Lord...   יְיָ מָלָךְ...

Speaking of God's holiness, and the laws of justice and morality which He has established, King David recalls Moses, Aaron, and Samuel to indicate that it was thanks to such leaders that the Jewish people were able to maintain their high standards of morality and justice.

We are reminded that the leaders and all the Jewish people are responsible to the same set of laws. Each and every Jew is equally obligated to fulfill the commandments of the Torah, regardless of his spiritual or political post.

A Psalm by David...   ...מִזְמוֹר לְדָוִד

Recited standing

This Psalm contains God's name 18 times. which is significant since it is the same as the numerical value of the Hebrew word *Chai*, Life.

The seven repetitions of the words *Kol Hashem*, Voice of the Lord, in this Psalm correspond to the seven days of Creation, when everything was created by God's word.

In the *kabbalah* (Jewish mysticism) we are told that a far-reaching and tremendous effect takes place in the Upper worlds when this Psalm is recited with concentration and joy.

Transliteration:

Mizmor l'dövid, hövu la-donöy b'nay aylim, hövu la-donöy kövod

44

vö-oz. Hövu la-donöy k'vod sh'mo hishtachavu la-donöy b'had'ras kodesh. Kol adonöy al hamö-yim, ayl ha-kövod hir-im, adonöy al ma-yim rabim. Kol adonöy bako-ach, kol adonöy be-hödör. Kol adonöy shovayr arözim, va-y'shabayr adonöy es ar'zay hal'vönon. Va-yarkidaym k'mo aygel, l'vönon v'siryon k'mo ven r'aymim. Kol adonöy chotzayv lahavos aysh. Kol adonöy yöchil midbör, yöchil adonöy midbar ködaysh. Kol adonöy y'cholayl a-yölos va-yechesof y'öros u-v'haychölo, kulo omayr kövod. Adonöy lamabul yöshöv, va-yayshev adonöy melech l'olöm. Adonöy oz l'amo yitayn, adonöy y'vöraych es amo va-shölom.

We implore you...   אָנָּא, בְּכֹחַ...

Recited standing. It is customary to recite this paragraph silently.

This is a very holy and mystical prayer. The prayer consists of 7 lines, each consisting of 6 words. The total number of words, 42, signify one of the mystical Divine names which has the same numerical value.

The 7 lines symbolize the 7 Divine Attributes (wisdom, kindness, severity, etc.) by means of which God rules the world.

The number 6 also has a deep mystical meaning. It is related to the six wings of the angels Isaiah saw in his prophetic vision. The *Shema*, the verse in which we pronounce God's unity, also contains 6 words of this paragraph.

While the average worshiper is not expected to delve into all the mysteries of the Kaballah, everyone is expected to know, at least, the meaning of the words.

Come, my Beloved...   ...לְכָה דוֹדִי

Recited standing

This beautiful hymn welcomes the Shabbat Queen. The refrain of this hymn *Lecho Dodi* and, indeed, the entire motif of the hymn, in which the Shabbat is represented as a "Queen" whom we go out to welcome, is based on a Talmudic source, where we are told how two great Sages went out to welcome the Shabbat Queen in this fashion.

Transliteration:

L'chöh dodi lik'ras kalöh, p'nay shabbös n'kab'löh. L'chöh dodi lik'ras kalöh, p'nay shabbös n'kab'löh.

Shömor v'zöchor b'dibur echöd, hishmi-önu ayl ha-m'yuchöd, adonöy echöd u-sh'mo echöd, l'shaym u-l'sif-eres v'lis'hilöh. L'chöh dodi lik'ras kalöh, p'nay shabbös n'kab'löh.

Lik'ras shabbös l'chu v'nayl'chöh, ki hi m'kor ha-b'röchöh, may-rosh mikedem n'suchöh sof ma-aseh b'macha-shövöh t'chilöh. L'chöh dodi lik'ras kalöh, p'nay shabbös n'kab'löh.

Hisna-ari may-öför kumi, liv'shi big'day sif-artaych ami, al yad ben yishai bays ha-lachmi, kör'vöh el nafshi g'ölöh. L'chöh dodi lik'ras kalöh, p'nay shabbös n'kab'löh.

46

Hisor'ri hisor'ri, ki vö oraych kumi ori, u-ri u-ri shir da-bayri, k'vod adonöy öla-yich niglöh. L'chöh dodi lik'ras kalöh, p'nay shabbös n'kab'löh.

Lo say-voshi v'lo si-köl'mi, mah tish-tochachi u-mah te-he-mi, böch yeche-su ani-yay ami, v'niv-n'söh hö-ir al tilöh. L'chöh dodi lik'ras kalöh, p'nay shabbös n'kab'löh.

V'höyu lim'shisöh sho-sö-yich, v'röchaku köl m'val'ö-yich, yösis öla-yich elohö-yich, kim'sos chösön al kalöh. L'chöh dodi lik'ras kalöh, p'nay shabbös n'kab'löh.

Yömin u-s'mol tifrotzi, v'es adonöy ta-aritzi, al yad ish ben partzi, v'nis-m'chöh v'nögilöh. L'chöh dodi lik'ras kalöh, p'nay shabbös n'kab'löh.

Turn around, facing west, and say:

Bo-i v'shölom ateres ba-löh, gam b'rinöh (On **Festivals:** **b'simchöh**) u-v'tzöhölöh, toch emunay am s'gulöh, (**Bow right**) bo-i chalöh, (**Bow left**) bo-i chalöh, (Say silently a third time:) bo-i chalöh shabbös malk'sö. L'chöh dodi lik'ras kalöh, p'nay shabbös n'kab'löh.

A Psalm, a song...　　　　　　　מִזְמוֹר שִׁיר...

This Psalm celebrates the Shabbat day. A day on which we cease 'creating' as God did on the seventh day of creation. This means not doing any of 39 kinds of creative physical activities and their off-shoots, as listed in the Torah and explained in the Code of Jewish Law.

47

The Lord is King... יְיָ מָלָךְ...

This Psalm expresses the theme of God's sovereignty and strength.

Mourner's Kaddish

Recited standing

At specifically marked intervals during the prayers, when praying with a quorum of at least ten Jewish male adults, mourners recite this Kaddish.

Kaddish means "holy." It was composed, like most of our prayers, by the Men of the Great Assembly. It is based on the wording of Ezekiel's prophecy in which Kiddush Hashem, the sanctification of God's Name, is placed in the center of the national duty of Israel, upon which the deliverance of the Jewish nation was dependent.

The word *Amen*, that the congregation responds, is like the word *Emunah*, which means belief, and by stating it we acknowledge that we believe what the reader has stated.

Transliteration:

Yis-gadal v'yis-kadash sh'may raböh.

(Cong: Ömayn)

B'öl'mö di v'rö chir'u-say v'yamlich mal'chusay, v'yatzmach pur'könay vikörayv m'shi-chay.

(Cong: Ömayn)

B'cha-yay-chon u-v'yomaychon u-v'cha-yay d'chöl bays yisro-ayl, ba-agölö u-viz'man köriv v'im'ru ömayn.

(Cong: Ömayn. Y'hay sh'mayh rabö m'vörach l'ölam u-l'öl'may öl'ma-yö, yisböraych.)

Y'hay sh'mayh rabö m'vörach l'ölam u-l'öl'may öl'ma-yö. Yisböraych, v'yishtabach, v'yispö-ayr, v'yisromöm, v'yis-nasay, v'yis-hadör, v'yis-aleh, v'yis-halöl, sh'may d'kudshö b'rich hu.

(Cong: Ömayn)

L'aylö min köl bir'chösö v'shirösö, tush-b'chösö v'neche-mösö, da-amirön b'öl'mö, v'im'ru ömayn.

(Cong: Ömayn)

Y'hay sh'lömö rabö min sh'ma-yö, v'cha-yim tovim ölaynu v'al köl yisrö-ayl v'im'ru ömayn.

(Cong: Ömayn)

Take three steps back: Oseh shölom (Between Rosh HaShonoh and Yom Kippur substitute: ha-shölom) bim'romöv, hu ya-aseh shölom ölaynu v'al köl yisrö-ayl, v'im'ru ömayn. Take three steps forward.

(Cong: Ömayn)

Just as they...   כְּגַוְנָא דְאִנּוּן...

This is a profoundly mystical, *kabbalistic*, passage, difficult to explain adequately here, especially since it is only a small section of a larger context. Suffice to say it describes the Divine attributes as they evolve with the approach of the Shabbat.

~~~~~~

The Friday Evening Services

The evening prayer consists of the *Shema* with two blessings before and two after it; the *Amidah*, special Shabbat portions and concluding prayers.

And say...   וְלוֹמַר בָּרְכוּ...

Recited only when praying alone, without a Minyan

This selection is recited when praying alone, without a Minyan (quorum) of ten male Jewish adults over the age of 13. It is meant to replace the *Bor'chu* call to prayer, which can only be recited with a Minyan.

Half Kaddish and *Bor'chu*

The Shabbat services continue here. Weekday Festival services begin here. (When the Festival occures on Shabbat, the services begin earlier with *Mizmor L'dövid*, 'A Psalm by David'.)

The leader recites Half Kaddish followed by *Bor'chu*.

The prayer of *Bor'chu* is a summons, or call, by the leader to join him in praising God. It is explained in *kabbalah*, that all *mitzvot* require proper preparation; we do not want to perform the sacred *mitzvot* without proper mental preparation. We take time to pause and think of the great significance of the mitzvah we are about to perform.

This same benediction is said once again at the end of the Shabbat evening prayer, for those who have tarried in coming to the synagogue (they were occupied preparing for the Shabbat) and have not heard its first recital.

***Bor'chu* is recited standing. When we say the words, we bow in reverence to the One and Only God.**

⚑ **Transliteration:**

When the leader says: *Bor'chu*... respond with the following verse. After he repeats it you may be seated:

Böruch adonöy Ha-m'voröch L'olöm Vö-ed.

Blessed are You...   ...בָּרוּךְ אַתָּה

Recited Seated

This is the first blessing before the *Shema*. It is similar in content to the blessing preceding the morning *Shema*.

With this blessing we acknowledge the awesome change from day to night. The opening verse refers to the first evening which God created, as it is written in Genesis, "And it was evening, and it was morning, one day."

What may seem as a 'natural' and 'ordinary' change from day to night, and from night to day; from summer to winter, and from winter to summer, and so on, is really a wonderful act of Creation by God. Not something to be taken for granted.

With everlasting...   ... אַהֲבַת עוֹלָם

This blessing is a fitting introduction to the *Shema*. It speaks of God's love to us, His people, and reminds us that the Torah and Mitzvot are not merely additions to our life, but our very life and only cause for existence.

Hear, O Israel... שְׁמַע יִשְׂרָאֵל...

The *Shema* is the essence of our faith. It consists of three paragraph taken from the Bible. The first paragraph begins with the proclamation: "The Lord is One." It goes on to tell us that we must love God and dedicate our lives to carrying out of will. We can keep this faith alive only if we bring up our children in this belief. This section also contains the two mitzvot of *Tefillin* and *Mezuzah*, which remind us that we are Jews.

The second chapter contains a promise that if we fulfill and observe God's commands we shall be a happy people in our land. If not, we will suffer exile and hardships in strange lands, so that by suffering and trouble we will learn the ways of God and return to Him. We are again reminded to teach our children our true faith, and the *Tefillin* and *Mezuzah* are again mentioned, because they are the symbols of practical observance of God's commands.

The third chapter contains the commandment of *Tzitzit*, the distinctive Jewish garment which is a constant reminder of all the precepts of the Torah. We are reminded, also, that God brought us out of Egypt and made us His people, and that we accepted Him as our God.

Transliteration:

It is customary to cover our eyes with our right hand while reciting the first verse of the *Shema*, in order to promote deep concentration.

Sh'ma yisrö-ayl adonöy elohaynu adonöy echöd.

Remove your hand from your eyes, and say the following in an undertone:

Böruch shaym k'vod mal'chuso l'olöm vö-ed.

Continue with a regular voice below:

V'öhavtö ays adonöy elohechö, b'chöl l'vöv'chö, u-v'chöl naf-sh'chö, u-v'chöl m'odechö. V'hö-yu ha-d'vörim hö-ayleh asher önochi m'tzav'chö ha-yom al l'vö-vechö. V'shinan-töm l'vönechö v'dibartö böm, b'shiv-t'chö b'vaysechö, u-v'lech-t'chö vaderech, u-v'shöch-b'chö, u-v'kumechö. U-k'shartöm l'os al yödechö, v'hö-yu l'totöfos bayn aynechö. U-ch'savtöm al m'zuzos bay-sechö, u-vish'örechö.

Truth and belief...   ‫...אֱמֶת וֶאֱמוּנָה‬

This section refers to the *Shema* we just read. It reinforces our connection and belief in God and recounts the numerous miracles He has wrought for the Jewish people which enabled us to be here today.

Who is like You...   ...מִי כָמוֹכָה

This prayer continues the themes of the preceding prayers. In it we proclaim the uniqueness of God, and make reference to the redemption that God has brought – and continues to bring – to the Jewish people.

Transliteration:

Mi chö-mochöh bö-aylim adonöy, mi kö-mochö ne-dör ba-kodesh, norö s'hilos, osay fele. Mal'chus'chö rö-u vönechö, bokay-a yöm lif'nay mo-sheh, zeh ayli önu v'öm'ru, adonöy yimloch l'olöm vö-ed. V'ne-emar, ki födöh adonöy es ya-akov, u-g'ölo mi-yad chözök mimenu. Böruch atöh adonöy gö-al yisrö-ayl.

Our Father, let us...   ...הַשְׁכִּיבֵנוּ אָבִינוּ

It is interesting to note that in this prayer we refer to God as "our Father," but upon waking in the morning we address Him as "our King." The reason for this is that in the course of the day we have learned from all that has happened to us that God has been more than a King to us; He has shown us many kindnesses and has taken care of us like a loving father.

And so, when we are about to retire for the night, we feel confident and secure in God, as a child feels secure in the arms of his father.

The Amidah

Blessed are You...   ...בָּרוּךְ אַתָּה

Recited standing, with feet together

We rise for the *Amidah*, the prayer in which we put forth our personal requests to God. We take three steps back, and then three steps forward, as if approaching a king. At the word *Boruch*, blessed, we bend the knee; *Atoh*, You, we bow forward; and at *Adonoy*, Lord, we straighten up.

The benedictions of the Amidah are as old as our people, and date back to the times of Abraham, Isaac and Jacob. But the final form of it, as we know it in our Prayer books, dates back to a later time, that of Ezra the Scribe and the Men of the Great Assembly more than 2,300 years ago. This was during the time of the Babylonian Exile, when the Jews were driven from their land into Babylon. Many began to forget the Hebrew language. It was then that the leaders and prophets of Israel — the Men of the Great Assembly — arranged the prayers in their fixed order, in Hebrew. Thus all the Jews, at all times and in all places would be reciting the same holy prayers, in the same language, and this would give them a feeling of unity and strength.

This prayer is also known as the *Shemone Esrei*, which means "eighteen," because originally this prayer had eighteen blessings (weekday version). These blessings and passages are more than a collection of petitions or requests for ourselves and our people. They also remind us of certain events in our history. According to our Sages, each blessing of the *Shemone Esrei* tells a story of some miracle that happened in the past, and on that occasion the blessing was said by the angels.

You have consecrated...   אַתָּה קִדַּשְׁתָּ...

This paragraph is a form of introduction to the quotation from the Torah where the Shabbat was first instituted. The words, "You sanctified the Seventh Day...You blessed it..." are in direct reference to the passage in the Torah.

The Sages of the Great Assembly formulated the text of this prayer to emphasize the holiness of Shabbat, at the same time alluding to the word kiddushin, "betrothal." God betrothed, so to speak, the Shabbat to the Jewish people.

What does it mean in practical terms that God sanctified the Shabbat unto His Name? It means that the Shabbat is more than a rest day, when man is to rest from his physical work; nor is it a day merely for socializing, or for ordinary enjoyment and recreation with the family. It has a higher purpose; it is different from all days and seasons. It is a day of holiness, of prayer and of Torah study. It is dedicated to God. Thus it brings a complete change from everyday life.

Shabbat is holier than any other day of the year. On the Shabbat, when properly observed, the Jew reaches the highest degree of completeness that any creature of God can ever reach. That is why the Shabbat is the end and purpose of the entire Creation, for when man reaches that height, he "justifies" the Creation, and God is pleased with His great handiwork.

The heavens...   ...וַיְכֻלּוּ הַשָּׁמַיִם

As *Rashi*, the classic commentator on the Torah, explains, mortal man cannot know the time exactly; this is one of the reasons why we usher in the Shabbat 18-20 minutes before sunset. But God knows the time exactly, and He finished and stopped from all His work "by the Seventh Day."

In reality God does not have to "rest," for He never gets tired. Although Shabbat, in this portion, is translated as "a day of rest," it really means a day of stoppage from all manner of "work." The Hebrew word used here in the Torah is not *avodah* which is work in the sense of any kind of labor that requires a physical effort. The word here is *melachah* which has quite a different meaning, and includes acts which require no effort. To strike a match or turn the electric switch requires no effort, yet it is forbidden on the Shabbat just like tilling the soil, or bricklaying, as mentioned earlier.

58

When we observe the Shabbat properly, we are living witnesses who testify by our way of life that God is the Creator of the World.

Our Sages tell us that when a person recites this passage in the Friday evening prayer with proper intent, the two angels accompanying him place their hands on his head and say, "Your sin is departed and your transgression is forgiven."

Those who observe...   יִשְׂמְחוּ...

In general it may be said that this prayer is almost like a paraphrase of the preceeding one. The wording of it, however, as in all prayers, is carefully chosen and meaningful.

Rejoicing is usually associated with our Festivals, but it also applies to Shabbat. Observing the Shabbat and keeping it holy brings us the sure promise of being satiated – gratified to the point of rejoicing – with God's goodness, both in this world and in the World To Come.

God called the Seventh day "Desirable of Days." This means that while the Six Days of Creation were necessary to create the world, it is the Seventh Day that God really desired and made holy. In our life, too, living as we are in a material world, we are expected to work and toil during the six days of the week, but these days are not an end in themselves: they are but a means to attain a higher form of living, to rise to a state of holiness. This is personified by Shabbat.

Our God...   אֱלֹהֵינוּ...

Examining the text of this prayer, we can see that it refers to both the "passive" and "active" aspects of Shabbat. As a day of rest from all work, we observe it simply by not doing any of the forbidden 39 kinds of work and their offshoots. This is the so-called "passive" aspect of Shabbat, and is referred to in this prayer by the words "accept with favor our (Shabbat) rest." At the same time, Shabbat has its "active" aspect, in that it is dedicated to mitzvot and the study of Torah.

This is why the prayer continues with the words "sanctify us with Your commandments and grant us a portion in Your Torah." This refers to the fact that every Jew has a portion and share in the Torah. It may be impossible for every person to study and master the whole Torah, but no matter on what level of understanding, every Jew has a portion in the Torah. By studying Torah every day to the best of one's ability, one takes possession of one's very own 'share' in the Torah. In this way, all Jews collectively share in the whole Torah.

Look with favor...   רְצֵה יְיָ...

This prayer begins the closing section of the Amidah. If Shabbat occures on Rosh Chodesh, we add a special prayer, following the paragraph above, and then resume the regular prayers.

At *Modim*, 'We thankfully Acknowledge...' we gently bow with the first words of this prayer.

The Amidah is concluded by taking three steps back, as if departing from the presence of a King, at the verse *Oseh Sholom*, 'He who makes the peace', and forward at the end of the verse.

The heavens...   ...וַיְכֻלּוּ הַשָּׁמַיִם

Recited standing

These verses are from the first chapter in Genesis. By reciting them a Jew gives testimony that God created the heavens and the earth, and all that is in them, in six days, and rested on the seventh day, which He proclaimed a holy day of rest.

As we mentioned before, the Jewish people are the living witnesses that attest to this truth, and every Jew should realize the great and unique privilege to be such a witness. Hence the *Zohar* concludes: "A Jew should give this testimony with joy and gladness of heart."

Transliteration:

Va-y'chulu hashöma-yim v'hö-öretz v'chöl tz'vö-öm. Va-y'chal elohim ba-yom hash'vi-i, m'lachto asher ösöh, va-yishbos ba-yom hash'vi-i miköl m'lachto asher ösöh. Va-y'vörech elohim es yom hash'vi-i, va-y'kadaysh oso, ki vo shövas miköl m'lachto, asher börö elohim la-asos.

He was a shield...   ...מָגֵן אָבוֹת

Recited standing

The words "He was a shield," "He resurrects the dead" and "the holy King" clearly refer to the familiar first three blessings of the Amidah. The words "for to them He decided to give rest" refer to the central Shabbat blessing, "please find favor in our rest." The words "We will serve Him," "God worthy of praise" and "Master of Peace" refer to the familiar last three blessings of every Amidah.

The leader follows this portion with a whole Kaddish.

Transliteration:

Mögayn övos bid'vöro m'cha-yeh maysim b'ma-amöro hö-ayl (between Rosh Hashana and Yom Kippur substitute: ha-melech) haködosh she-ayn kömohu ha-mayni-ach l'amo b'yom shabbas ködsho, ki vöm rötzöh l'höni-ach löhem, l'fönöv na-avod b'yir'öh vö-fachad v'nodeh lish'mo b'chöl yom tömid, may-ayn hab'röchos, ayl ha-hodö-os adon ha-shölom, m'kadaysh ha-shabbös u-m'vöraych sh'vi-i, u-mayni-ach bik'dushöh, l'am m'dush'nay oneg, zaycher l'ma-asay v'rayshis.

A Psalm by David... מִזְמוֹר לְדָוִד...

Recited standing

This Psalm is one of the most familiar of the Book of Psalms. It is also one of the most beautiful and comforting. The whole serene picture of peace and comfort, free from anxiety and fear, plus a feeling of closeness to God – all this reflects the Shabbat atmosphere.

It is incumbent... עָלֵינוּ...

Recited standing. (Between Pesach and Shavuot, the *Omer* is counted here.)

Our Sages tell us that this prayer was composed by Joshua, as he led the children of Israel into the Promised Land. And if you look carefully you will find that the initials taken from the first letter of each sentence in the first paragraph, read backwards, form his name "Hoshua."

Thus, when Joshua was about to settle the Jewish people in the Holy Land, he made them remember, through this hymn, that they were different from the Canaanite peoples and other nations and tribes of the earth, who "worship vain things and emptiness."

Transliteration:

Ölaynu l'shabay-ach la-adon hakol, lösays g'dulöh l'yotzayr b'rayshis, shelo ösönu k'go-yay hö-arötzos, v'lo sömönu k'mish-p'chos hö-adömöh, shelo söm chelkaynu köhem, v'gorölaynu k'chöl ha-monöm sehaym mishtachavim l'hevel v'lörik. Va-anachnu kor'im u-mishtachavim u-modim, lif'nay melech, mal'chay ha-m'löchim, ha-ködosh böruch hu. She-hu noteh shöma-yim v'yosayd öretz, u-moshav y'köro ba-shöma-yim mima-al, u-sh'chinas u-zo b'göv'hay m'romim, hu elohaynu ayn od. Emes malkaynu, efes zulöso, kakösuv b'soröso. V'yöda-tö ha-yom vaha-shayvosö el l'vövechö, ki adonöy hu hö-elohim ba-shöma-yim mima-al, v'al hö-öretz mi-töchas, ayn od.

V'al kayn n'kaveh l'chö adonöy elohaynu lir-os m'hayröh b'sif-eres u-zechö, l'ha-avir gilulim min hö-öretz v'hö-elilim köros yiköray-sun, l'sakayn olöm b'mal'chus shadai, v'chöl b'nay vösör yik-r'u vish'mechö, l'hafnos ay-lechö köl rish-ay öretz. Yakiru v'yayd'u köl yosh'vay sayvayl, ki l'chö tichra köl berech, tishöva köl löshon. L'fönechö adonöy elohaynu yich-r'u v'yipolu, v'lich'vod shim'chö y'kör yitaynu vi-kab'lu chulöm alayhem es ol mal'chusechö, v'simloch alayhem m'hayröh l'olöm vö-ed, ki ha-mal'chus shel'chö hi, u-l'ol'may ad timloch b'chövod, ka-kösuv b'soRösechö, adonöy yimloch l'olöm vö-ed. V'ne-emar, v'hö-yöh adonöy l'melech al köl hö-öretz, ba-yom hahu yih-yeh adonöy echöd u-sh'mo echöd.

Mourner's Kaddish

Recited standing

At the conclusion of *Olaynu*, when praying with a quorum of at least ten Jewish male adults, mourners recite this Kaddish.

🎵 **Transliteration:**

Yis-gadal v'yis-kadash sh'may raböh.

(Cong: Ömayn)

B'öl'mö di v'rö chir'u-say v'yamlich mal'chusay, v'yatzmach pur'könay vikörayv m'shi-chay.

(Cong: Ömayn)

B'cha-yay-chon u-v'yomaychon u-v'cha-yay d'chöl bays yisro-ayl, ba-agölö u-viz'man köriv v'im'ru ömayn.

(Cong: Ömayn. Y'hay sh'mayh rabö m'vörach l'ölam u-l'öl'may öl'ma-yö, yisböraych.)

Y'hay sh'mayh rabö m'vörach l'ölam u-l'öl'may öl'ma-yö. Yisböraych, v'yishtabach, v'yispö-ayr, v'yisromöm, v'yis-nasay, v'yis-hadör, v'yis-aleh, v'yis-halöl, sh'may d'kudshö b'rich hu.

(Cong: Ömayn)

L'aylö min köl bir'chösö v'shirösö, tush-b'chösö v'neche-mösö, da-amirön b'öl'mö, v'im'ru ömayn.

(Cong: Ömayn)

Y'hay sh'lömö rabö min sh'ma-yö, v'cha-yim tovim ölaynu v'al köl yisrö-ayl v'im'ru ömayn.

(Cong: Ömayn)

Take three steps back: Oseh shölom (Between Rosh HaShonoh and Yom Kippur substitute: ha-shölom) bim'romöv, hu ya-aseh shölom ölaynu v'al köl yisrö-ayl, v'im'ru ömayn. Take three steps forward.

(Cong: Ömayn)

Do not fear...   ...אַל תִּירָא

Recited standing

These meaningful verses express an important message to us as we conclude the service and are about to part ways.

They remind us that no matter how long our exile may be, or what fears and anxieties beset us, God will always 'carry' us. We are God's 'burden' and responsibility, and God will never drop this burden. He will surely deliver us from our enemies and from the exile.

✏ Transliteration:

Al tirö mipachad pis-om, u-misho-as r'shö-im ki sövo. U-tzu aytzöh v'suför, dab'ru dövör v'lo yökum, ki imönu ayl. V'ad zik-nöh ani hu, v'ad sayvöh ani esbol, ani ösisi va-ani esö, va-ani esbol

66

va-amalayt. Ach tzadikim yodu lish'mechö yay-sh'vu y'shörim es pö-nechö.

Kaddish D'rabonon

Recited standing

This is a special prayer for the Rabbis, scholars and students of the Torah. It is recited by a mourner at the conclusion of the services.

 Transliteraion:

Yis-gadal v'yis-kadash sh'may raböh.

(Cong: Ömayn)

B'öl'mö di v'rö chir'u-say v'yamlich mal'chusay, v'yatzmach pur'könay viköräyv m'shi-chay.

(Cong: Ömayn)

B'cha-yay-chon u-v'yomaychon u-v'cha-yay d'chöl bays yisro-ayl, ba-agölö u-viz'man köriv v'im'ru ömayn.

(Cong: Ömayn. Y'hay sh'mayh rabö m'vörach l'ölam u-l'öl'may öl'ma-yö, yisböraych.)

Y'hay sh'mayh rabö m'vörach l'ölam u-l'öl'may öl'ma-yö. Yisböraych, v'yishtabach, v'yispö-ayr, v'yisromöm, v'yis-nasay, v'yis-hadör, v'yis-aleh, v'yis-halöl, sh'may d'kudshö b'rich hu.

(Cong: Ömayn)

L'aylö min köl bir'chösö v'shirösö, tush-b'chösö v'neche-mösö, da-amirön b'öl'mö, v'im'ru ömayn.

(Cong: Ömayn)

Al yisrö-ayl v'al rabönön, v'al tal-midayhon, v'al köl tal-miday sal-midayhon, v'al köl mön d'ös'kin b'oray'sö. Di v'asrö hödayn, v'di v'chlö asar v'asar. Y'hay l'hon u-l'chon shlömö rabö, chinö v'chisdö v'rachamin v'cha-yin arichin, u-m'zonö r'vichö u-fur'könö min ködöm avu-hon div'sh'ma-yö v'im'ru ömayn.

(Cong: Ömayn)

Y'hay sh'lömö rabö min sh'ma-yö, v'cha-yim tovim ölaynu v'al köl yisrö-ayl v'im'ru ömayn.

(Cong: Ömayn)

Take three steps back: Oseh shölom (Between Rosh HaShonoh and Yom Kippur substitute: ha-shölom) bim'romöv, hu ya-aseh shölom ölaynu v'al köl yisrö-ayl, v'im'ru ömayn. Take three steps forward.

(Cong: Ömayn)

-This concludes the evening services-

The Shabbat Morning Services

We begin the morning service with the same introductory prayers as on weekday mornings. These are recited prior to the communal services in the synagogue. In these prayers we recount our thanks to God for giving us another day of life.

The prayers also recount the daily sacrifices and services in the Holy Temple which stood in Jerusalem over 2,000 years ago. The reason for this is to remind us that the material creations of this world can and should be used to serve a higher purpose, unlike other beliefs that state that physical aspects of this world are 'evil' in essence and have no redeeming factors.

The order of the morning service is as follows:

1. Psalms for the Shabbat.

2. Verses of praise.

3. The Blessings of *Shema*, and the *Shema*.

4. The Amidah, silent prayer.

5. The reading of the Torah.

6. The Musaf service.

7. Concluding prayers.

We begin the service with twelve Psalms which are added to the Shabbat service. Ten of these allude to the ten sayings by which God created the world. These opening prayers are mostly devoted to the expression of thanks for God's help and grace.

One of the reasons why these Psalms are added is to distinguish this day from the rest of the week, furthermore because the people do not have to go to work and there is no hardship for people to spend some more time in the synagogue.

Offer praise...   ...הוֹדוּ לַיְיָ

The first part of this prayer comes from the first book of Chronicles. King David composed this prayer, and the famous singer Asaph and his choir sang it in the Sanctuary on the day when the Holy Ark was returned to Jerusalem.

The second section, which begins with *Shiru La-hashem*, Sing to the Lord, and ends with *V'hallel La-hashem*, and praise to the Lord, was said in the Temple every evening, right after the completion of the offerings. It pictures the future as promised to us in the holy Scriptures, when God will be recognized by all of mankind, and the Jews will be respected as the true servants of God.

A Psalm, a song...   ...מִזְמוֹר שִׁיר

The name of God is mentioned ten times in this Psalm, alluding to the ten commandments. King David composed this Psalm for the dedication of the Holy Temple in Jerusalem. It is also a prophecy for the future Temple which will be built by Moshiach.

Today, in the absence of the Holy Temple, our synagogues are called 'Miniature Sanctuaries'. Our services in the synagogue replace, for now, the Divine services in the Holy Temple.

As we begin our prayers we have full confidence that our prayers will be heard. This theme is found in this Psalm as well.

The Lord is King...   ...יְיָ מֶלֶךְ

Recited standing

The central theme of these passages is God's reign upon all the earth. Thus, while we recognize our good fortune in that God has been especially gracious to us in bringing us close to Him, we hope and pray for the day when all the nations of the world will also acknowledge God and fear Him. After this is said, you may be seated.

For the Choirmaster...   ...לַמְנַצֵּחַ מִזְמוֹר

This Psalm includes the theme of creation: The heavens and earth, day and night, the rising sun – each proclaiming the glory of God as it manifests itself in the 'natural' order and beauty of the created universe.

71

Notice the connection between God, Torah, and man. As we are taught by our Sages, God created the world for the sake of the Torah and for the sake of the Jewish people.

Sing joyously...   ...רַנְּנוּ צַדִּיקִים

This Psalm continues the expression of thanks to God for creating the world. Recognizing the order and system with which God runs the world. Nothing is random. All is directed by the all capable God.

To say that God is too big to care for every tiny creature is to place limitations on He who is infinite and limitless. It is because He is *not* limited to the confines of a worldly existence that He can concern himself with the minutest details of every blade of grass and each cell in our bodies.

Therefore, to place our trust in mere worldly items is like mistaking the forest for the trees. It is God to whom we must turn and place our trust in Him, following the way of life He set forth for us in the Torah.

A Psalm by David...   ...לְדָוִד בְּשַׁנּוֹתוֹ

This Psalm follows the order of the Hebrew alphabet. Beginning with the second verse, each verse starts with a new letter.

King David wondered why God created insanity. David wondered what good evolves for anyone, when a man walks in the street, tears at his clothes, and children run after him and taunt him!

God said to him, "A time will come when you will need it and pray for it!" Indeed, when David fled from King Saul to the King of Achish, the brother of Goliath sought to avenge his brother's blood, being the body guard of King Achish.

David prayed to God for some 'insanity' to disguise his fame. And this was how he saved himself. David then composed this Psalm to indicate that one should praise God in times of well being as well as in times of distress. And all that God does is for the good.

King David goes on to tell us that our relationship with God is something which needs to be 'tasted', meaning experienced. Just like a fine delicacy one cannot know what it tastes like by reading about it, or hearing its description. So too is our personal experience with God. It is the *actual observance* of His precepts in everyday life that provides the taste and real feeling of Godliness in one's life.

A prayer by Moses...   תְּפִלָּה לְמֹשֶׁה...

According to tradition, this is the first of eleven Psalms composed by Moses. King David incorporated them into his Book of Psalms along with other Psalms composed by various authors (including Solomon, Asaph, Heyman, Eitan (Abraham), and the sons of Korach).

73

The designation "Man of God" in the beginning of the Psalm suggests that Moses did not insert this description of himself, but King David did to identify and describe the author.

The theme of this Psalm is *teshuva*, repentance. In Hebrew the word *teshuva* really means return. When a Jewish person commits a sin, either by commission or omission, he creates a 'separation' between himself and God, the Source of Life. This 'partition' can be removed by sincere repentance, through resolving to recommit ourselves to His Torah, and abandoning our sinful ways. So in essence we are returning to where we were originally, before the initial sin.

Shabbat is associated with *teshuva* because on Shabbat our soul, being released from its material 'shackles', is able to freely 'return' to it's heavenly source for these 26 hours (which is also the numerical value of God's name). Indeed, the Hebrew word of Shabbat and *teshuva* share the exact same letters, שבת - תשב.

You who dwells...   ישֵׁב בְּסֵתֶר...

Our Sages tell us that Moses recited this Psalm when he went up to Mount Sinai.

In this Psalm we learn that the person who puts his complete trust in God will certainly find himself secure and safe under His 'shadow.'

A Psalm. Sing... מִזְמוֹר שִׁירוּ...

This Psalm speaks of the Messianic era. King David acclaims God's wondrous acts when the time will come to reveal His might and glory.

During the long and dark exile, the nations of the world mocked and derided the Jewish people, saying that God has forgotten and forsaken them, and they could be persecuted without fear of punishment. But those wicked nations are due to find out how wrong they were, as we note here in this Psalm.

A Song of Ascents... שִׁיר לַמַּעֲלוֹת...

The main theme of this Psalm is God's benevolent providence. Sometimes on the brink of despair, a person may wonder, "From where will my help come?" But the person who believes in God will immediately feel reassured, for, however 'hopeless' the situation may seem, surely there isn't anything that God cannot do. Indeed, King David assures us that God will not let down those who put their faith in Him.

The notion of God's 'guardianship' is mentioned six times. This underlines that God's protection is needed each and every day of the work week, while the holy seventh day, Shabbat, is in itself especially blessed with God's protection and peace.

A Song of Ascents...   שִׁיר הַמַּעֲלוֹת...

This Psalm is dedicated to the holy city of Jerusalem. Here Kind David expresses his acknowledgement that the reason he and his men were successful in defending the Jewish people against their enemies, was due to the 'gates' and upholders of Jerusalem, meaning the places where Torah scholars gathered to study and expound the Torah. In other words, in the merit of the Yeshiva students studying Torah, the defending forces were successful in the battlefield.

The relevance of this Psalm to Shabbat is that what Jerusalem is in terms of holiness and peace in 'space', Shabbat is in terms of holiness and peace in 'time'. And both, rooted in God's Torah and mitzvot, are the eternal bonds that unite and unify all Jews.

A Song of Ascents...   שִׁיר הַמַּעֲלוֹת...

According to our Sages, 'lifting up one's eyes to Heaven' is more than a gesture of prayer. It means that one should see and understand that the cause of everything is in Heaven.

A Song of Ascents...   שִׁיר הַמַּעֲלוֹת...

This Psalm continues the theme of our dependence on God at all times, especially in times of trouble. Trouble could also be spiritual. When we fail to live up to the way of life outlined in the Torah, and fall short in in our service to God, we too should pray to Him for Divine assistance to pull us through. As our Sages tell us, One who comes to be purified, is helped from above.

Praise the Lord...   הַלְלוּיָהּ הַלְלוּ...

Recited standing

This Psalm begins a series of praises to God. His might, His compassion and His glory.

Upon closer examination of the first verse we may wonder why are we enjoined to offer praise to the servants of the Lord as well? To this, our Sages reply, that by respecting those who follow Torah and adhere closely to its *mitzvot,* we will ultimately learn from them, and follow in their ways.

Praise the Lord...   הוֹדוּ...

Recited standing

Our Sages explain that the 26 verses of praise to God in this prayer allude to the 26 generations of the human race that preceded the giving of the Torah at Mount Sinai.

Since the world was created for the sake of the Torah, and

without Torah it could not have existed on its own merits, the world was sustained during this period entirely by God's boundless kindness.

The 26 generations (2,448 years) comprise the ten generations from Adam to Noah; another ten from Noah to Abraham; and the next six generations, namely, Isaac, Jacob, Levi, Kehot, Amram and Moses.

Transliteration:

Hodu la-adonöy ki tov, ki l'olöm chasdo.

Hodu lay-lohay hö-elohim, ki l'olöm chasdo.

Hodu la-adonay höadonim, ki l'olöm chasdo.

L'osay niflö-os g'dolos l'vado, ki l'olöm chasdo.

L'osay ha-shöma-yim bi-s'vunöh, ki l'olöm chasdo.

L'roka hö-öretz al ha-mö-yim, ki l'olöm chasdo.

L'osay orim g'dolim, ki l'olöm chasdo.

Es ha-shemesh l'mem-sheles ba-yom, ki l'olöm chasdo.

Es ha-yöray-ach v'cho-chövim l'memshlos ba-löyla, ki l'olöm chasdo.

L'makay mitzra-yim biv'choray-hem, ki l'olöm chasdo.

Va-yotzy yisrö-ayl mitochöm, ki l'olöm chasdo.

B'yöd chazököh u-viz'roah n'tuyöh, ki l'olöm chasdo.

L'gozayr ya suf lig'zörim, ki l'olöm chasdo.

V'he-evir yisrö-ayl b'socho, ki l'olöm chasdo.

V'ni-ayr par'oh v'chaylo v'yam suf, ki l'olöm chasdo.

L'molich amo bamidbör, ki l'olöm chasdo.

L'makay m'löchim g'dolim, ki l'olöm chasdo.

Va-yaharog m'löchim adirim, ki l'olöm chasdo.

L'sichon melech hö-emori, ki l'olöm chasdo.

U-l'og melech ha-böshön, ki l'olöm chasdo.

V'nösan artzöm l'na-chalöh, ki l'olöm chasdo.

Na-chalöh l'yisrö-ayl avdo, ki l'olöm chasdo.

Sheb'shiflaynu zöchar lönu, ki l'olöm chasdo.

Va-yifr'kaynu mitzöraynu, ki l'olöm chasdo.

Nosayn lechem l'chöl bösör, ki l'olöm chasdo.

Hodu l'ayl ha-shömö-yim, ki l'olöm chasdo.

Power and...

הָאַדֶּרֶת וְהָאֱמוּנָה...

Recited standing

This hymn follows the Hebrew alphabetical order. According to our Sages, it is recited by the angels in heaven while singing the praises of God. The general meaning of this hymn is that all the attributes that can be enumerated are true only when applied to God. But when they are applied to mortal human beings, they cannot be true, because a human being has a limited life on earth and all his qualities are necessarily limited and imperfect.

Therefore, the power of a human king or ruler is only temporary; the trustworthiness of a person is unreliable; a person's circumstance might change, his understanding is limited, his knowledge incomplete. All this should cause every person to feel very humble — certainly when he stands before God!

Transliteration:

Hö-aderes v'hö-emunah, l'chai olömim.

Ha-binöh v'ha-b'röchöh, l'chai olömim.

Ha-ga-avöh v'hag'dulöh, l'chai olömim.

Ha-day-öh v'hadibur, l'chai olömim.

Ha-hod v'he-hödör, l'chai olömim.

Ha-va-ad v'ha-vösikus, l'chai olömim.

Ha-ziv v'ha-zohar, l'chai olömim.

Ha-chayil v'ha-chosen, l'chai olömim.

Ha-teches v'ha-tohar, l'chai olömim.

Ha-yichud v'ha-yiröh, l'chai olömim.

Ha-keser v'ha-kövod, l'chai olömim.

Ha-lekach v'ha-libuv, l'chai olömim.

Ha-m'luchöh v'ha-memshölöh, l'chai olömim.

Ha-noy v'ha-naytzach, l'chai olömim.

Ha-siguy v'hasegev, l'chai olömim.

Hö-oz v'hö-anövöh, l'chai olömim.

Ha-p'dus v'ha-p'ayr, l'chai olömim.

Ha-tzvi v'ha-tzedek, l'chai olömim.

Ha-k'ri-öh v'ha-k'dushöh, l'chai olömim.

Hö-ron v'höro-maymos, l'chai olömim.

Ha-shir v'ha-shevach, l'chai olömim.

Ha-t'hilöh v'ha-tiferes, l'chai olömim.

For the sake of...   ...לְשֵׁם יִחוּד

Recited standing

It is explained in *kabbalah*, that all mitzvot require proper preparation. We do not want to perform the sacred mitzvot without proper mental preparation. We take time to pause and think of the great significance of the mitzvah we are about to perform.

Men gather their two front *Tzitzit* in their left hand, in preparation for the following blessing, and hold them through its conclusion.

Blessed is He...   ...בָּרוּךְ שֶׁאָמַר

Recited standing

This blessing continues the theme of gratitude we began at the beginning of the services with *Hodu*. Men hold the *Tzitzit* to remember before Whom we are speaking.

We describe God's different attributes and manifestations to become more aware and 'acquainted' with Him, in order to praise Him more wholeheartedly in the following Psalms.

After the blessing men kiss the *Tzitzit*, to express their endearment to the mitzvot.

82

Transliteration:

Böruch she-ömar v'hö-yöh hö-olöm, böruch hu, böruch omayr v'oseh, böruch gozayr u-m'ka-yaym, böruch oseh v'rayshis, böruch m'ra-chaym al hö-öretz, böruch m'ra-chaym al ha-b'ri-yos, böruch m'shalaym söchör tov liray-öv, böruch chai lö-ad v'kayöm lö-netzach, böruch podeh u-matzil, böruch sh'mo. Böruch atöh adonöy elohaynu melech hö-olöm, hö-ayl, öv höracha-mön, ha-m'hulöl b'feh amo, m'shuböch u-m'fo-ör bil'shon chasidöv va-avödoöv, u-v'shi-ray dövid av-dechö. N'ha-lelchö adonöy elohaynu, bish'vöchos u-viz'miros. N'gadel'chö u-n'shabay-chacö u-n'fö-er'chö, v'namlich'chö v'nazkir shim'chö malkaynu elohaynu, yöchid, chay hö-olömim, melech. M'shuböch u-m'fo-ör, aday ad sh'mo ha-godol. Böruch atöh adonöy, melch m'hulöl batish-böchos.

Men kiss the *Tzitzit* (fringed garment). From this time until the conclusion of the Amidah, we refrain from speaking.

A Psalm, a song...   מִזְמוֹר שִׁיר...

Recited standing

This Psalm celebrates the Shabbat day. A day on which we cease 'creating' as God did on the seventh day of creation. This means not doing any of 39 kinds of creative physical activities and their off-shoots, as listed in the Torah and explained in the Code of Jewish Law.

The Lord is king...

יְיָ מָלָךְ...

Recited standing

This Psalm expresses the theme of God's sovereignty and strength. After this pslam is recited, you may be seated.

May the glory...

יְהִי כְבוֹד...

This hymn is a compilation of different passages from various Psalms. It is a prelude to the Verses of Praise that immediately follow.

It contains 21 names of God, just as many as there are sentences in the next Psalm, *Ashrei*. The ideas mentioned, of God's mercy and loving care, serve as a fitting introduction to the next prayer.

Happy are those...

אַשְׁרֵי יוֹשְׁבֵי...

Our Sages tell us that whoever says this Psalm three times a day will have a share in the world to come. Indeed, it is incorporated into the daily prayers so that by praying each day, we recite this Psalm three times.

Each verse begins with a letter from the Hebrew alphabet (except the letter נ which is included in the next verse). This is to express that we praise God with all possible forms of human expression.

Transliteration:

Ash-ray yosh'vay vaysechö od y'hal'luchö selöh. Ash-ray hö-öm sheköchö lo, ash-ray hö-öm she-adonöy elohöv. T'hilöh l'dövid aromi-m'chö elohai ha-melech, va-avör'chöh shim'chö l'olöm vö-ed. B'chöl yom avör'chechö, va-ahal'löh shim'chö l'olöm vö-ed. Gödol adonöy u-m'hulöl m'od, v'lig'dulöso ayn chayker. Dor l'dor y'shabach ma-asechö, u-g'vurosechö yagidu. Hadar k'vod hodechö, v'div'ray nifl'osechö ö-sichöh. Ve-ezuz nor'osechö yomayru, u-g'dulös'chö a-sap'renöh. Zecher rav tuv'chö yabi-u, v'tzid'kös'chö y'ra-naynu. Chanun v'rachum adonöy, erech apa-yim u-g'döl chösed. Tov adonöoy lakol, v'ra-chamöv al köl ma-asöv. Yoduchö adonöy köl ma-a-sechö, va-chasi-dechö y'vör'chucöh. k'vod mal'chus'chö yomayru, u-g'vurö-s'chö y'da-bayru. L'hodi-ah liv'nay hö-ödöm g'vurosöv, u-ch'vod hadar mal'chuso. Mal'chus'chö, mal'chus köl olömim, u-memshalt'chö b'cöl dor vödor. Somaych adonöy l'chöl hanof'lim, v'zokayf l'chöl hak'fufim. Aynay chol aylechö y'sa-bayru, v'atöh nosayn löhem es öchlöm b'ito. Posay-ach es yödechö, u-masbi-a l'chöl chai rötzon. Tzadik adonöy b'chöl d'röchöv, v'chösid b'chöl ma-asöv. körov adonöy l'chöl kor'öv, l'chol asher yikröu-hu ve-emes. R'tzon y'ray-öv y-aseh, v'es shav'ösöm y'shma v'yoshi-aym. Shomayr adonöy es köl ohavöv, v'ays köl hör'shö-im yashmid. T'hilas adonöy y'daber pi, vivörAych köl bösör shaym köd'sho l'olöm vö-ed. Va-anachnu n'voraych yöh, may-atöh v'ad olöm ha-l'luyöh

Praise the Lord...   הַלְלוּיָהּ הַלְלִי...

This and the next four paragraphs are taken from the final Psalms in the Book of Psalms.

Here, king David speaks for the Jews as he praises God for His help, disavowing all trust in human strength and power. Human help is but temporary, and rarely unselfish. God's help, however, is eternal and dependable. it comes to the poor and rich alike. It supports the orphaned and the widowed and protects the just from the unjust.

Notice how this Psalm begins in the singular form, and slowly, over the next four Psalms, progresses to a thundering climax, as the entire universe shouts out praise to God.

Praise the Lord...   הַלְלוּיָהּ כִּי טוֹב...

This Psalm turns to the 'communal' Divine Providence. God's special care for the Jewish people is expressed in relation to His order and rule of nature. Just as nature is under His control and will, so too are the Jewish People.

Praise the Lord...   הַלְלוּיָהּ הַלְלוּ...

In this Psalm the entire universe is put aflame with the glory of the Creator. Heaven and earth and all their hosts join in one mighty chorus of God's glory.

Praise the Lord...   ...הַלְלוּיָהּ שִׁירוּ

This Psalm concludes with a vision of the future. Where all the world — not just the Jewish People and the whole of nature — will recognize God, and sing His praise. King David sees this as a time when the whole world will resemble one big Temple that resounds with a great new song of praise.

Praise the Lord...   ...הַלְלוּיָהּ הַלְלוּ

In this final Psalm, all voices unite in this beautiful hymn, where we glorify God in all ways, especially with these 13 expressions of glory. This is a befitting introduction to the culmination of our prayers in the *Shema* and the *Amidah* that follow.

Transliteration:

Ha-l'luyöh. Ha-l'lu ayl b'köd'sho, ha-l'luhu bir'kiah u-zo. Ha-l'luhu big'vurosöv, ha-l'luhu k'rov gud'lo. Ha-l'luhu b'sayka shoför, ha-l'luhu b'nayvel v'chinor. Ha-l'luhu b'sof u-möchol, ha-l'luhu b'minim v'ugöv. Ha-l'luhu b'tzil-tzlay shöma, ha-l'luhu b'tzil-tzlay s'ruöh. kol ha-n'shömöh t'halayl yöh ha-l'luyöh, kol ha-n'shömöh t'halayl yöh ha-l'luyöh.

Blessed is the Lord...

בָּרוּךְ יְיָ...

Recited standing

This prayer begins the final sections of the Verses of Praise portion of our morning prayers. We rise for this prayer and remain standing for the next few passages, emphasizing its importance, and to follow the example of King David and the prophet Nehemia who were standing out of honor when they recited it as well.

And David blessed...

וַיְבָרֶךְ דָּוִיד...

Recited standing

All the previous chapters of the Verses of Praise were intended to help us understand the glory and power of God, and were all leading up to the following prayers, in which the meaning of all blessings is clearly stated – the realization that we owe everything to God.

When King David felt his last days had come, he gathered all the princes of Israel and the captains of his host and, in a final farewell, blessed the Lord before all the congregation. It is these moving words that we recite here. We also recap our formation as a people, and remember the very foundations of our faith.

Jewish Faith in God means a great deal more than "faith" in its ordinary meaning. Faith implies complete, blind acceptance of something not supported by reason. Where people see and hear something with their own eyes and ears, they do not need to have "faith" in the existence of that thing.

Similarly, the Jewish people, having seen with their own eyes the Divne revelations at the Crossing of the Red Sea, did not have to rely on "faith" to believe in God; they knew and experienced God's Presence, for they saw God's "Mighty Hand" as it triumphed over Pharaoh and the Egyptians. This is why each and every one of them could sing: "This is my God and I will glorify Him"– as one points to something before his very eyes, and as we will recite in the next prayer.

It is this personal experience, which the children of Israel of that generation conveyed to the next generation, and that one to the next, that was transmitted from father to son to the present day; transmitted uninterruptedly, and by thousands upon thousands of men and women, since there has never been a break in Jewish history from as far back as the time of Abraham to this day.

It follows that, in reciting the passages from the Torah about the Exodus from Egypt in our daily morning prayer, we do not merely recount that important historical event, but also reaffirm our trust in God.

Then Moses...   אָז יָשִׁיר מֹשֶׁה...

Recited standing

The great events of the Exodus from Egypt were marked by extraordinary miracles and wonders. It was after witnessing the Divine revelations at the *Yam Suf* (the Red Sea), that the children of Israel attained the highest degree of awe and fear of God and, at the same time, a profound trust in God and in Moses, His servant. Thereupon, Moses and the children of Israel were inspired to sing the *Shira* (song), known as the Song at the Sea.

The saintly *Shaloh* and other authorities point out that this prayer should be said standing, and with joy, as if we ourselves are actually standing at the shore of the *Yam Suf* and singing it with Moses. It should also evoke feelings of intense trust in God.

The verse "The Lord will reign for ever and ever" is repeated twice, indicating that the Song ends here. Then follows the Aramaic version of this verse, and several other verses. The theme of these verses is the future and final redemption of our people, and the great Divine revelation which will usher in the Messianic era when "On that day God will be One, and His Name One," that is to say, when God's unity will be recognized by all, not just the Jewish people.

The soul of...   ...נִשְׁמַת כָּל חַי

Recited standing

This beautiful and inspiring prayer is only recited on the Shabbat and Festivals, because on the Shabbat and Yom Tov we abstain from work and have more time to recite longer prayers.

It is one of the oldest of our prayers. It is mentioned in the Talmud and various Sages are named as its author, among them, *Shimon Ben Shetach.* It is a hymn of praise to God, and its main theme is the miracle of the liberation from Egypt. That is why it is said immediately after the "Song of Moses." That is also why our Sages sometimes call this prayer *Birchat Hashir,* the Blessing of the Song.

The various expressions of God's help in this prayer, are used not just for style. God's help comes in many different ways. Sometimes, when Jews are threatened, God punishes and destroys their enemies. At other times God brings about a change of heart in these wicked people. The Egyptians and Pharaoh are an example of the first kind of deliverance, the story of Purim is an illustration of the way God brought about a change of heart in King Ahasuerus, who himself eventually ordered the hanging of Haman.

Similarly there are different kinds of troubles that face our people: sometimes it is a *tzarah,* a threatened calamity, that everyone can see; sometimes it is a *metzukah,* an inner plight not always apparent to all, yet perhaps even more dangerous. In every case, God, who leads His world with kindness and His creatures with mercy, takes care of us. Sometimes we may not even be aware of any threat. God, however, knows, for He watches over every one of us.

God is infinitely kind, and it is in His very nature to do good. If our fate were always entirely decided by our own virtues and merits, who could be sure of his future? But we rely on God's mercy and kindness. And as long as we try to live according to His Will, we can be confident of God's help. That is why we want to thank God constantly for the great favors that He bestows upon us.

This prayer should not be said in a hurry; we ought to think deeply about God's kindness to us, and how we owe everything to Him. If we would but realize this, we would never stop singing God's praises, not only with our soul and breath, but with every part and limb of our body.

He who dwells...   שׁוֹכֵן עַד...

Recited standing

With this paragraph the thoughts and expressions of the above prayers culminate, and is followed with the closing blessing of the Verses of Praise.

And therefore...   ...וּבְכֵן יִשְׁתַּבַּח

Recited standing

This is the closing blessing of the Verses of Praise. In this prayer we find fifteen expressions of praise. The number fifteen has a deep significance. The numerical value first two Hebrew letters of God's name, *Yud* and *Hey*, equal fifteen. The number fifteen is also related to the fifteen Psalms that the Levites recited as they ascended the fifteen steps leading to the Sanctuary.

The prayer concludes with the words "Life of [all] the worlds." We have been praising God, His might, wisdom and kindness; we have extolled Him as the Creator of everything that exists and breathes. But He is not merely the Creator of these things; He is the very life of all these things. He is the origin of life and He is life — the never-ending and never-resting energy and driving force of the whole universe.

🏳 **Transliteration:**

Yishtabach shim'chö lö-ad malkaynu, hö-ayl, ha-melech, ha-gödol v'haködosh, ba-shöma-yim u-vö-öretz. ki l'chö nö-eh adonöy elohay-nu vay-lohay avosaynu l'olöm vö-ed. Shir u-sh'vöchöh, ha-layl v'zimröh, oz u-memshölöh, netzach, g'dulöh u-g'vuröh, t'hilöh v'sif-eres, k'dushö u-mal'chus. B'röchos v'hodö-os, l'shim'chö

93

ha-gödol v'ha-ködosh u-mayolöm ad olöm, atöh ayl. Böruch atöh
adonöy, ayl melech, gödol u-m'hulöl batshböchos, ayl ha-hodö-os,
adon ha-niflö-os boray köl ha-n'shömos, ribon köl ha-ma-asim,
ha-bochayr b'shiray zimröh, melch yöchid chay hö-olömim.

A Song of Ascents... שִׁיר הַמַּעֲלוֹת...

Recited standing, and only on the Shabbat preceding Yom kippur.

This Psalm reflects the spirit of repentance during the High
Holidays.

Half Kaddish and *Bor'chu*

The leader recites Half kaddish followed by *Bor'chu*.

The prayer of *Bor'chu* is a summons, or call, by the leader to join
him in praising God. It is explained in *kabbalah*, that all *mitzvot*
require proper preparation; we do not want to perform the sacred
mitzvot without proper mental preparation. We take time to pause
and think of the great significance of the mitzvah we are about to
perform.

***Bor'chu* is recited standing. When we say the words, we bow in reverence
to the One and Only God.**

Transliteration:
When the leader says: *Bor'chu...* **respond with the following verse. After he repeats it you may be seated:**

Böruch adonöy Ha-m'voröch L'olöm Vö-ed.

Blessed are You...   בָּרוּךְ אַתָּה...

This is the first blessing before the *Shema*. With this blessing we acknowledge the awesome change from day to night. The opening verse refers to the first evening which God created, as it is written in Genesis, "And it was evening, and it was morning, one day."

What may seem as a 'natural' and 'ordinary' change from day to night, and from night to day; from summer to winter, and from winter to summer, and so on, is really a wonderful act of Creation by God.

All shall praise you...   הַכֹּל יוֹדוּךְ...

That God is the Creator of the world is something we must remember every day, and constantly bear in mind. It is only then that we can truly declare that God is One, as we say in the *Shema*. That is why the *Shema* is introduced by the following prayers and blessings.

This particular prayer begins with a declaration that all created things praise God. Not only man, but everything that God created is evidence of God's greatness and holiness. God is "holy" in the sense that He is beyond our understanding; for He is the Creator of everything, human beings and angels alike, and no created being, not even an angel, can understand God.

Moving from praising God, we now thank God for the kindness and mercy with which He constantly takes care of the whole universe. To the Creator of the world and merciful King we address our petition for mercy and for our very existence and life.

We conclude this section of the prayer by saying that there is none to equal God, nor is there anything except God. By this we mean that in spite of the wonderful world we live in, with the majestic sun and other heavenly bodies, there is nothing that has any semblance to, or comparison with, the Creator Himself. Moreover, since everything depends upon the Creator for its very existence and life, there is, in the final analysis, nothing but the Creator Himself.

Finally, we mention the four worlds that span our destiny: this world that we live in; the "next" world, after life on this earth (a purely spiritual world of the souls); the period when Moshiach will come, when our people will be restored to their former glory in the Holy Land; and finally, the time when the dead will be resurrected and this world will attain its highest perfection.

In mercy He gives...　　　הַמֵּאִיר לָאָרֶץ...

Recited only on Festivals which fall on weekdays.

In this prayer we praise God for creating and giving us light. While other people might take it for granted, we Jews are grateful to God for giving light to the inhabitants of the Earth. Moreover, we realize that there is Divine mercy in the way He bestows His gifts upon us.

For example, there is a slow and gradual transition from night to day and from day to night. This gives us a chance to get used to the light and heat of the sun. Similarly, the sun does not disappear without warning, so that we can adjust ourselves to the night.

All shall praise You...　　　אֵל אָדוֹן...

This is a prayer-poem written in alphabetical order. It is a hymn of praise to God, the Master of all creatures, and it was composed alphabetically to illustrate that the world was created by the word of God and for the sake of the Torah, written in the twenty-two letters of the Hebrew alphabet.

It is interesting to note that the first two verses have five words each, a total of ten words corresponding to the ten commands with which the world was created. The next eighteen verses have four

97

words each, totaling seventy-two, corresponding to the highest numerical combination of the Divine Name. The last two verses have six words each, totaling twelve, corresponding to the number of constellations, which is quite appropriate, as they speak of the "heavenly hosts," that is, the stars.

Transliteration:

Ayl ödon al köl ha-ma-asim, böruch u-m'voröch b'fi köl ha-n'shömöh, göd'lo v'tuvo mölay olöm, da-as u-s'vunöh sov'vim hodo.

Ha-mis-göeh al chayos ha-kodesh, v'nehdör b'chövod al ha-merkövöh, z'chus u-mishor lif'nay chis-o, chesed v'rachamim mölay ch'vodo.

Tovim m'oros, sheböröh elohaynu, y'tzöröm b'da-as b'vinoh u'v'haskayl, ko-ach u-g'vuraöh nösan böhem, li-h'yos mosh'lim b'kerev tay-vayl.

M'lay-im ziv u-m'fikim nogah, nöeh zivom b'chöl hö-olöm, s'maychim b'tzaysöm v'sösim b'vo-öm, osim b'aymöh r'tzon konöm.

P'ayr v'chövod nos'nim l'sh'mo, tzö-hölöh v'rinöh l'zaycher mal'chuso, körö la-shemesh va-yizrach or, rö-öh v'hiskin tzuras hal'vönöh.

Shevach nosh'nim lo köl tz'vo mörom, tif-eres u-g'dulöh, s'röfim v'chayos v'ofa-nay ha-kodesh.

The the Almighty... לָאֵל אֲשֶׁר שָׁבַת...

This prayer is a direct continuation of the previous prayer. It is a prayer of praise to God who created the Shabbat as a day of rest.

Having created the world, including man, in the six days of Creation, God was exalted and He, anthropomorphically, ascended and sat upon His throne. Before the Creation, there was no one to call Him king, and no one to practice benelovence to. But now God was truly the king, with the whole Creation, and especially man, to acknowledge His Divine majesty. For this occasion God robed Himself in beauty. "Beauty" (in Hebrew, *tiferet*) is the quality of justice tempered with mercy.

This is the Divine "robe," for He rules the world with justice, mingled with mercy. Were He to rule the world with stern justice alone, it would be difficult for any creature to justify its existence, and hence the world could not exist. In His kindness, God tempered stern justice with mercy, so that the sinner will not be immediately destroyed, but have a chance to better himself, and God will forgive him.

Be eternally blessed... תִּתְבָּרֵךְ לָנֶצַח...

This prayer vividly describes how the heavenly angels offer their praises to God. It is natural for us to turn from the luminaries to the angels in Heaven. For as we look up to the sky and marvel at God's Creation, we look further into Heaven and "behold" the angels worshipping God in trembling fear and awe.

The picture so vividly drawn before our eyes by the great prophets Isaiah and Ezekiel is awe-inspiring, and goes a long way to preparing us for the great prayer of *Shema*.

The Name...   ...אֶת שֵׁם

When mentioning the yoke of Heavenly kingship, it should be noted that a yoke is put on animals not for the purpose of torturing them, but to enable them to pull together in harmony.

In the same way we speak of the "yoke of the Kingdom of heaven" in relation to ourselves. It means that not only must we accept the sovereignty of God, but that we should all "pull together" to further God's reign upon the earth. We wear this yoke willingly and joyfully, knowing that the precepts and commands of God, far from enslaving us, give us real spiritual freedom and unlimited power and control over the passions and weaknesses of our human nature.

Holy, holy...   ...קָדוֹשׁ קָדוֹשׁ

There is a great deal of preparation going on among the angelic hosts before they utter their prayers to sanctify their Creator.

Kadosh means "separate"; to say that God is holy is to say that God is separated from, and unaffected by, the world He created. The repetition of the word "holy" three times is explained in the Aramaic translation of the Kedusha in the prayer of *U-va L'tzion*: "Holy in the heavens above, the abode of His glory; holy on earth, the work of His might; holy forever and ever."

Transliteration:

Ködosh, ködosh ködosh, adonöy tzivö-os, m'lo chöl hö-öretz k'vodo.

Blessed be the glory...   ...בָּרוּךְ כְּבוֹד

Here too we have a prayer uttered by the angels, who proclaim God's praise with a mighty sound.

Transliteration:

Böruch k'vod adonöy mim'komo.

They chant sweet...   ...לָאֵל בָּרוּךְ

This is the last section of the first blessing before the *Shema*. As is the case of long blessings, which concluded with a similar thought as they begin, this blessing begins and concludes with the idea that God has never stopped for a moment the process of creation.

We bless God as the creator of the "luminaries." Here we have in mind not only the physical lights, the light of the sun and moon and other forms of illumination, but also "lights" in a deeper sense, the light of the Torah and its mitzvot, as it is written "A mitzvah is a lamp, and the Torah is light."

Lord our God...   אַהֲבַת עוֹלָם...

This is the second of the two blessing that come before the *Shema*. It is a perfect, final introduction.

The opening words of this prayer speak of God's love and kindness in giving us the Torah. We pray that just as God has taught our ancestors the laws of life, He should be gracious and give us proper understanding of His teachings as well.

The sentences that follow contained the wishes and prayers that mean most to every Jew: that God grant us understanding "To obey, learn, and teach, to keep, practice, and uphold all the words of instruction in Your Torah." It is not only for ourselves that we pray, but also for children, and for all the Jewish people.

It customary that during the second to the last sentence of this prayer, to have in mind the following five items: The giving of the Torah; God's bringing us to Mount Sinai; the incident with *Amalek* (see, Exodus); the story with Miriam (see, Exodus); and the Shabbat.

The first and last word of this moving prayer is love. We are moved by the unending love which God has shown us from the days of Abraham, as we have seen through all the prayers until this point.

🏴 **Transliteration:**

...Övinu öv hörachamön, ham'rachaym, rachem nö ölaynu, v'sayn b'libaynu binöh l'hövin ul'haskil, lishmo-a lilmod ul'lamayd, lishmor v'la-asos, ul'ka-yaym es köl div'ray sal-mud torösechö b'ahavöh. V'hö-ayr aynaynu b'sorösechö, v'dabayk libaynu b'mitzvosechö, v'yachayd l'vövaynu l'ahavöh ul'yiröh es sh'mechö...

Towards the end of this blessing, men gather all four Tzitzit in their left hand, and hold it throughout the Shema.

Hear, O Israel...   ...שְׁמַע יִשְׂרָאֵל

The *Shema* is the essence of our faith. It consists of three paragraphs taken from the Bible. The first paragraph begins with the proclamation: "The Lord is One." It goes on to tell us that we must love God and dedicate our lives to carrying out of will. We can keep this faith alive only if we bring up our children in this belief. This section also contains the two mitzvot of *Tefillin* and *Mezuzah*, which remind us that we are Jews.

The second chapter contains a promise that if we fulfill and observe God's commands we shall be a happy people in our land. If not, we will suffer exile and hardships in strange lands, so that by suffering and trouble we will learn the ways of God and return to Him. We are again reminded to teach our children our true faith, and the *Tefillin* and *Mezuzah* are again mentioned, because they are the symbols of practical observance of God's commands.

The third chapter contains the commandment of *Tzitzit*, the distinctive Jewish garment which is a constant reminder of all the precepts of the Torah. We are reminded, also, that God brought us out of Egypt and made us His people, and that we accepted Him as our God.

Transliteration:

It is customary to cover our eyes with our right hand while reciting the first verse of the *Shema*, in order to promote deep concentration.

Sh'ma yisrö-ayl adonöy elohaynu adonöy echöd.

Remove your hand from your eyes, and say the following in an undertone:

Böruch shaym k'vod mal'chuso l'olöm vö-ed.

Continue with a regular voice below:

V'öhavtö ays adonöy elohechö, b'chöl l'vöv'chö, u-v'chöl

naf-sh'chö, u-v'chöl m'odechö. V'hö-yu ha-d'vörim hö-ayleh asher önochi m'tzav'chö ha-yom al l'vö-vechö. V'shinan-töm l'vönechö v'dibartö böm, b'shiv-t'chö b'vaysechö, u-v'lech-t'chö vaderech, u-v'shöch-b'chö, u-v'kumechö. U-k'shartöm l'os al yödechö, v'hö-yu l'totöfos bayn aynechö. U-ch'savtöm al m'zuzos bay-sechö, u-vish'örechö.

It is customary that when saying the word Tzitzit, and Emet, (in the third paragrpah of the Shema) for men to kiss the Tzitzit.

Truth and certain...   ...אֱמֶת, וְיַצִּיב

This prayer is the continuation of the theme of the blessing preceding the *Shema*. It begins a series of 16 words which are closely related to the concept of truth, emphasizing the truthfulness of all that we declared in the *Shema*. The 16 expressions are said to refer to the 16 verses in the first two sections of the *Shema*.

This prayer speaks of God's eternal faithfulness to the Jewish people, of the great love which he has shown to us throughout the ages, by liberating our ancestors from Egypt, and continuing to be our "Shield of deliverance" in the most difficult of times.

From the first...   ...עַל הָרִאשׁוֹנִים

This prayer continues the theme of the preceding prayer. We also emphasize the eternity of the Torah. No matter what day and age we find ourselves in, the Torah remains relevant and pure.

You have always...	...עֶזְרַת אֲבוֹתֵינוּ

In this prayer we summarize all we have mentioned above, and prepare for the Amidah.

With a new song...	...שִׁירָה חֲדָשָׁה

This prayer leads directly to the Amidah. We are not to make any interruptions between them, but proceed with the Amidah.

The Amidah

Blessed are You...	...בָּרוּךְ אַתָּה

Recited standing, with feet together

In the order of our prayers, the Amida comes fourth. We have had (1) the blessings upon rising from bed; (2) the chapters of praise; (3) Shema; and now (4) The Amidah. (On Festivals a special Amidah is substituted.)

We rise for the Amidah, the prayer in which we put forth our personal requests to God. We take three steps back, and then three steps forward, as if approaching a king. At the word *Boruch*, blessed, we bend the knee; *Atoh*, You, we bow forward; and at *Adonoy*, Lord, we straighten up.

The benedictions of the Amidah are as old as our people, and date back to the times of Abraham, Isaac and Jacob, but the final form of it, as we know it in our Prayer books, dates back to a later time, to the time of Ezra the Scribe and the Men of the Great Assembly more than 2,300 years ago. That was the time of the Babylonian Exile, when the Jews were driven from their land into Babylon. Many began to forget the Hebrew language. It was then that the leaders and prophets of Israel — the Men of the Great Assembly — arranged the prayers in their fixed order, in Hebrew.

Thus all the Jews, at all times and in all places would be reciting the same holy prayers, in the same language, and this would give them a feeling of unity and strength.

This prayer is also known as the *Shemone Esrei*, which means "eighteen," because originally this prayer had eighteen blessings (weekday version). These blessings and passages are more than a collection of petitions or requests for ourselves, and our people. They also remind us of certain events in our history. According to our Sages, each blessing of the Shemone Esrei tells a story of some miracle that happened in the past, which was the first occasion when the blessing was said by the angels.

Moses rejoiced...   יִשְׂמַח מֹשֶׁה...

This prayer commences the special central blessing of the Shabbat Amidah. We remember Moses for it was he who introduced Shabbat to the Jewish people. It was also on Shabbat that the Torah was given.

And the children...   וְשָׁמְרוּ...

This is one of the well-known Biblical passages in which the Torah speaks of the Shabbat.

The first aspect of Shabbat observance is not to do any of the 39 categories of work (with their offshoots) that would desecrate (make unholy) the Shabbat. But that is not enough; we must do many things to consecrate (make holy) the Shabbat. These include — in addition to the pre-Shabbat preparations — such specific Mitzvot as lighting the candles before sunset, reciting the Shabbat prayers, making Kiddush, eating festive meals, devoting extra time to Torah study, etc.

"Throughout their generations" — means that the Shabbat must be kept at all times, and in all places; there is no exception whether we are in the desert, in the Land of Israel, or in America, and we must keep it today as did our ancestors a thousand years ago.

We are also obligated to see to it that our children and children's children will keep it to the end of days. We must make the Shabbat an everlasting covenant.

The word for covenant is Brit, and it reminds us of the Covenant of our father Abraham, circumcision. Just as circumcision is the covenant between our people and God, so is the Shabbat another sign of that covenant. The first is sealed in our body, and the second is sealed in our soul; no Jew is complete when one or the other is missing.

And you, Lord...　　　　　　　　...וְלֹא נְתַתּוֹ

This section is a continuation of the previous theme. The Shabbat is exclusively Jewish; no other nation in the world has a share in it, for it is the symbol of the loving relationship that exists between God and the Jewish People: God chose Israel and Israel chose God.

Those who observe...　　　　　　　...יִשְׂמְחוּ

In general it may be said that this prayer is almost like a paraphrase of the preceeding one. The wording of it, however, as in all prayers, is carefully chosen and meaningful.

Rejoicing is usually associated with our Festivals, but it also applies to Shabbat. Observing the Shabbat and keeping it holy brings us the sure promise of being satiated – gratified to the point of rejoicing – with God's goodness, both in this world and in the World To Come.

God called the Seventh Day "Desirable of Days." This means that while the Six Days of Creation were necessary to create the world, it is the Seventh Day that God really desired and made holy. In our life, too, living as we are in a material world, we are expected to work and toil during the six days of the week, but these days are not an end in themselves: they are but a means to attain a higher form of living, to rise to a state of holiness. This is personified by the Shabbat.

Our God...   ...אֱלֹהֵינוּ

Examining the text of this prayer, we can see that it refers to both the "passive" and "active" aspects of Shabbat.

As a day of rest from all work, we observe it simply by not doing any of the forbidden 39 kinds of work and their offshoots. This is the so-called "passive" aspect of Shabbat, and is referred to in this prayer by the words "accept with favor our (Shabbat) rest." At the same time, Shabbat has its "active" aspect, in that it is dedicated to Mitzvot and the study of Torah.

This is why the prayer continues with the words "sanctify us with Your commandments and grant us a portion in Your Torah." This refers to the fact that every Jew has a portion and share in the Torah.

It may be impossible for every person to study and master the whole Torah, but no matter on what level of understanding, one has a portion in the Torah. By studying Torah every day to the best of one's ability, one takes possession of one's very own 'share' in the Torah. In this way, all Jews collectively 'share' in the whole Torah.

Look with Favor...   רְצֵה יְיָ...

This prayer begins the closing section of the Amidah. (If the shabbat occurs on Rosh Chodesh, we add a special prayer right after the paragraph above, and then resume the regular prayers). At Modim, "We thankfully Acknowledge..." we gently bow with the first words of this prayer.

The Amidah is concluded by taking three steps back, as if departing from the presence of a king, at the verse *Oseh Sholom*, He who makes the peace, and three steps forward to complete the *Amidah*.

The Leader's Repetition of the Amidah.

A repetition of the Amidah is recited by the leader. This custom was set in place around the time of the formulation of the Amidah. The leader repeated the Amidah for those who could not read the Hebrew, having them in mind.

The Kedusha

Recited standing, with our feet together

This is a special sanctification prayer recited in unison during the repetition of the Amidah. The congregation recites one verse at a time, followed by the leader.

There is a great deal of preparation going on among the angelic hosts before they utter their prayers to sanctify their Creator: *Kadosh, kadosh, kadosh* ('Holy, holy, holy').

Kadosh also means "separate"; to say that "God is holy" is to say that God is separated from, and unaffected by, the world He created. The repetition of the word "holy" three times is explained in the Aramaic translation of the kedusha in the prayer of *U-va L'tzion*: "Holy in the heavens above, the abode of His glory; holy on earth, the work of His might; holy forever and ever."

While reciting this prayer, stand with your feet together and refrain from any interruption. Afterwards, you may be seated.

Transliteration:

Nak-dishöch v'na-aritzöch k'no-am si-ach sod sar'fay kodesh ha-m'shal'shim l'chö k'dushöh, ka-kösuv al yad n'vi-echö v'körö zeh el zeh v'ömar. Wait for leader.

Ködosh, ködosh, ködosh, adonöy tzivö-os, m'lo chöl hö-öretz

112

k'vodo. Öz b'kol ra-ash gödol adir v'chözok, mashmi-im kol, misna-s'im l'umas has'röfim, l'u-mösöm m'shab'chim v'om'rim. Wait for leader.

Böruch k'vod adonöy mim'komo. Mim'komöch malkaynu sofi-ah v'simloch ölaynu l'olöm vö-ed. Tishkon tisgadayl v'siska-daysh b'soch y'rushöla-yim ir'chö, l'dor vödor u-l'naytzach n'tzöchim. V'ay-naynu sir-enöh mal'chu-sechö, ka-dövör hö-ömur b'shiray u-zechö, al y'day dövid m'shi-ach tzidkechö. Wait for leader.

Yimloch adonöy l'olöm elohayich tziyon ldor vö-dor ha-l'luyöh. Wait for leader. You may be seated when the leader concludes the blessing.

The Modim

Recited standing, while the leader recites *Modim*.

[] **Transliteration:**

Modim anach-nu löch, shö-atöh hu adonöy elo-haynu vay-lohay avosaynu elohay köl bösör, yotz'raynu, yotzayr b'rayshis. B'röchos v'hodö-os l'shim'chö hagödol v'haködosh, al she-heche-yisönu v'kiyam-tönu. kayn t'cha-yaynu us'ka-y'maynu v'se-esof gölu-yosay-nu l'chatzros ködshechö, v'nösuv ay-lechö lishmor chukechö, v'la-asos r'tzonechö, ul'övd'chö b'layvöv shölaym, al she-önu modim löch. Böruch ayl ha-hodö-os.

113

Today is the...　　　　　　　　　　　　...הַיּוֹם יוֹם

After the repitition of the Amidah has been concluded, we recite the Psalm that corresponds to this day of the week. In the days of old, when the Holy Temple was in existence, the Levites had an important part in the holy service conducted there daily. Their task was to sing hymns of praise to God, which they also accompanied on musical instruments. One of the highlights of the service of the Levites was the singing of the "Song of the Day." It consisted of a special Psalm, a different one for each of the seven days of the week. This has been made part of our morning service.

On Rosh Chodesh and Festivals, special Psalms of praise called *Hallel*, is recited first.

A Psalm, a song...　　　　　　　　　　...מִזְמוֹר שִׁיר

This Psalm for the day of Shabbat celebrates the Shabbat day. A day on which we cease 'creating' as God did on the seventh day of creation. This means not doing any of 39 kinds of creative physical activities and their off-shoots, as listed in the Torah and explained in the Code of Jewish Law.

Deliver us...   הוֹשִׁיעֵנוּ יְיָ...

This passage is always recited after the Song of the Day, and serves as its closing.

Mourner's Kaddish

Recited standing

When praying with a quorum of at least ten Jewish male adults, mourners recite this Kaddish.

Transliteration:

Yis-gadal v'yis-kadash sh'may raböh.

(Cong: Ömayn)

B'öl'mö di v'rö chir'u-say v'yamlich mal'chusay, v'yatzmach pur'könay viközrayv m'shi-chay.

(Cong: Ömayn)

B'cha-yay-chon u-v'yomaychon u-v'cha-yay d'chöl bays yisro-ayl, ba-agölö u-viz'man köriv v'im'ru ömayn.

(Cong: Ömayn. Y'hay sh'mayh rabö m'vörach l'ölam u-l'öl'may öl'ma-yö, yisböraych.)

Y'hay sh'mayh rabö m'vörach l'ölam u-l'öl'may öl'ma-yö. Yisböraych, v'yishtabach, v'yispö-ayr, v'yisromöm, v'yis-nasay, v'yis-hadör, v'yis-aleh, v'yis-halöl, sh'may d'kudshö b'rich hu.

(Cong: Ömayn)

L'aylö min köl bir'chösö v'shirösö, tush-b'chösö v'neche-mösö, da-amirön b'öl'mö, v'im'ru ömayn.

(Cong: Ömayn)

Y'hay sh'lömö rabö min sh'ma-yö, v'cha-yim tovim ölaynu v'al köl yisrö-ayl v'im'ru ömayn.

(Cong: Ömayn)

Take three steps back: Oseh shölom (Between Rosh HaShonoh and Yom Kippur substitute: ha-shölom) bim'romöv, hu ya-aseh shölom ölaynu v'al köl yisrö-ayl, v'im'ru ömayn. Take three steps forward.

(Cong: Ömayn)

You have been showen...   ...אַתָּה הָרְאֵיתָ

Recited standing

Following the Song of the Day, several selected verses are recited by way of introduction to the order of the Torah reading.

The Torah Reading

The custom of reading sections from the Torah in the Congregation dates back to the time of Moses. We find that Moses assembled all the people and read them sections from the Torah pertaining to Shabbat and the Festivals. He also instituted that no three days should pass without a person hearing a Torah reading.

Later, Ezra the Scribe instituted and formalized the Torah readings for Mondays and Thursdays and other special days. Monday and Thursday were "market" days, when villagers came to town and had the opportunity to attend congregational services.

The Torah readings are generally as follows: On Shabbat the weekly portion is read, and seven male Jewish adults are "called up" to have a portion of the Sidra read to each. An eighth person is called up for *Maftir* and *Haftarah* (a chapter from the Prophets). At the *Minchah* (afternoon service) on Shabbat, the first part of next week's portion is read, and three people are called up. On Monday and Thursday, the same first part of the current Sidra is read, and three people are called up as well.

The reading of the Torah is most important, for the Torah is the holiest thing we possess; it is the wisdom of God, and contains the commandments God has given us and desires us to observe and fulfill in our everyday life.

Every time we take the Torah from the Ark, we are reminded of that great event when the Torah was first given to us by God on Mount Sinai. All the people stood and trembled in the presence of God.

It would be too much to expect of us to feel exactly the same way every time we see the Torah taken from the Ark, but at least something of those exciting feelings that our ancestors felt on that occasion should enter our heart and mind when the same Torah is taken out to be read to us. And so we stand up the moment the Ark is opened and say a short prayer which is a quotation from the Torah itself.

When the Torah is taken out, all the people have to come to attention with awe and trembling, and attune their hearts as if they are at that moment standing at Mount Sinai to receive the Torah. The Torah scroll will be brought from the ark to the reading table, where the reader will read the Torah portion of this week.

Whenever the Ark...   ...וַיְהִי בִּנְסֹעַ

Recited standing, as the ark is opened

As the ark is opened we recite this passage.

We bless God for having given us the Torah "with His holiness." The Torah and holiness are bound together. A holy way of life is one in which everything we do is dedicated to God. It is not a life of ease, but a life of service. God requires His people to be a "holy nation."

The Torah stresses: "You shall be holy; for I, your God, am holy." Thus, in the few words that comprise this short prayer, we bring up the past — Moses and the Ark; and the future — the day when all the earth will be filled with the knowledge of God. And the two are linked to the present – our dedication to the Torah in our present-day life.

🎺 **Transliteration:**

Va-y'hi bin'soa hö-öron va-yomer mosheh. Kumöh adonöy, v'yöfutzu oy'vechö, v'yönusu m'san'echö mi-pönechö. Ki mitzi-yon tay-tzay soröh, ud'var adonöy miru-shölö-yim. Böruch shenösan toröh l'amo yisrö-ayl bik'dushöso.

Blessed is the Name...   ...בְּרִיךְ שְׁמֵהּ

Recited standing

This deeply moving prayer is written in Aramaic, a language similar to Hebrew which was spoken in Babylon. The Talmud is also written in Aramaic, as also certain holy books (like the *Zohar*) and several other prayers.

This prayer is very old. It is first found in the *Zohar* (also known a the Book of *Kabbalah*). There it is stated: "Said Rabbi Shimon, 'When the Congregation takes out the Scroll of the Torah to read in it, the Heavenly Gates of Mercy are opened, and God's love is aroused. Then the following prayer should be said."

Thus we learn that the time of opening the Ark and taking out the Torah to read is a very special time, a time of Heavenly mercy and love, when our prayers are especially acceptable.

When we speak of God's "right hand" in this prayer, we mean God's might and power with which He protects us and redeems us from our enemies. When God let our Holy Temple (which stood in Jerusalem over 2,400 years ago) be destroyed, it is said, "He held back His right hand." Here we pray that God shows us once again His right hand and brings us salvation by rebuilding His Holy House.

We also pray to God to open our heart to His Torah, for there is an inborn love for the Torah in our heart, yet very often our heart is closed, and this love remains buried. We pray that God opens our heart, so that we become conscious of it and make it grow and overflow into our whole life.

We pray to God to fulfill our heart's desire "for good, for life and for peace." And "life" means more than just mere existence, but a life in accordance with Torah and Mitzvot. And "peace" also means more than the absence of war. It means true peace and inner harmony, which can be achieved only when the soul is master over the body, when our love for God and the Torah makes all contrary desires meaningless.

Transliteration:

...Bay anö röchitz, v'lish'may kadishö yakirö anö ay-mar

tushb'chön. Y'hay raava ködömöch d'siftach libö-i b'oray'sö, v'sashlim mish-alin d'libö-i, v'libö d'chöl amöch yisrö-ayl, l'tav u-l'cha-yin v'lish'löm.

Hear, O Israel...   שְׁמַע יִשְׂרָאֵל...

Recited standing

As the Torah is taken from the Ark, it is a most appropriate time to declare our faith in the One God, for the Torah is also one and only, holy and eternal. when the leader, who is our representative, makes this declaration while holding the Torah, and that we repeat it after him, it is like declaring it on oath.

While the Torah scroll is held, the leader recites the verse of *Shema* and *Echod*. We repeat each verse after him. The leader then recites *Gad'lu* and we follow with *L'cho Hashem*, Lord, Yours is the greatness, while the Torah is carried to the reading table.

Transliteration:

Wait for leader and repeat: Sh'ma yisrö-ayl adonöy elohaynu adonöy echöd.

Wait for leader and repeat: Echöd elohaynu, gödol ado-naynu, ködosh (v'norö) sh'mo.

Wait for leader and repeat: L'chö adonöy ha-g'dulöh v'hag'vuröh v'ha-tif-eres v'ha-naytzach v'ha-hod, ki chol bashöma-yim u-vö-öretz. L'chö adonöy ha-mam'löchöh v'ha-misnasay l'chol l'rosh. Rom'mu adonöy elohaynu v'hishtachavu la-hadom rag-löv ködosh hu. Rom'mu adonöy elohaynu v'hish-tachavu l'har köd-sho, ki ködosh adonöy elohaynu.

Reading the portion of the Week

The Torah is read. Seven Jewish men over the age of Bar Mitzvah (13) are called up to the Torah, one at a time, and honored with one seventh of the portion.

This is the Torah...   ...וְזֹאת הַתּוֹרָה

Recited standing

With the conclusion of the reading from the Torah, the Torah is lifted for all to see, and we recite this verse.

Here we are proudly stating that this is the same Torah which Moses placed before the children of Israel over 3,300 years ago. Nothing in it has changed. And it is as relevant today as it was then.

Transliteration:

V'zos ha-toröh asher söm mosheh lif'nay b'nay yisrö-ayl. Aytz cha-yim hi la-machazikim böh, v'som'chehö m'ushör. D'röchehö dar'chay no-am, v'chöl n'sivo-sehö shölom. Orech yömim bi-minöh bis'molöh osher v'chövod. Adonöy chöfaytz l'ma-an tzidko yagdil toröh v'ya-dir.

The *Haftorah*

The *Haftorah*, a selection from the Prophets, is read. This custom began over 2,400 years ago when the Romans forbade the public reading of the Torah. To compensate for this, the Rabbis chose portions from the Prophets that complemented or were similar to the Torah portion of that week. Thus the custom of reading from the Torah publiclly was not interupted, and the Romans were placated since they did not consider the Prophets part of the Bible.

May there come...   ‫...יְקוּם פֻּרְקָן‬

Recited standing

With the conclusion of the Haftorah, we recite this prayer, which is also written in Aramaic.

Since this prayer captures a glimpse of a fascinating era of our Jewish history that is not very well known, we will include here some additional historical information that will aid you in understanding it.

This prayer was introduced some fifteen hundred years ago in Babylon, soon after the completion of the Talmud. At that time the greatest Jewish center was in Babylon, and the prayer was written in Aramaic so that everybody should understand it.

At that time Jewish life in Babylon flourished. The Talmud was studied with great devotion and diligence in the great Yeshivot of Neharde'a, Sura and Pumbedita. The Jews enjoyed much freedom and independence, able to live their way of life as a separate community. They had the privilege of electing a descendant of the royal house of David as their representative before the Babylonian government. He was called "*Resh Galuta*" – Exilarch; or Head of the Exile, for the Jews never forgot that they were in exile there. All the Jews respected him greatly, and accorded him almost royal honor. He was regarded with great honor also among the dignitaries and officials of the government. He had a great deal of influence and power, and very often was also an outstanding Torah scholar. However, the real spiritual leaders of the people were the heads of the great Babylonian yeshivot who, after the completion of the Talmud, were called Rabbanan Seburai and (later) Geonim.

The yeshivot were very large at that time, for the study of Torah and Talmud was the most desired thing in those days. There were also head-teachers, called Rashei Kala, who presided over the annual assemblies that took place two months in the year, the Yarchei Kala. These were the months of Adar and Elul, when students and scholars from far and near joined the regular students, to review and revise what they had studied during the other months of the year. In addition there were also *Dayyanim* ("judges") who were members of the Beth Din (courts), before whom all disputes were brought for judgment and settlement. These were called *Dayyanei d'Vava* ("Judges at the Gates"). Now that we are familiar with these names and functions, we can fully appreciate this prayer.

Although this prayer was composed some fifteen hundred years ago, it is still valid for our times, for we, too, have spiritual leaders, rabbis and scholars, heads of yeshivot and students. We say this beautiful prayer for them every Shabbat, for we realize that upon their welfare depends the welfare of our people as a whole. And as we pray for them, we are reminded of our obligation to support them and the yeshivot, for by supporting them and enabling them to devote all their time to the study of the Torah, we become their partners and have a share in the Torah which they learn. Thus we are also included among "all those who occupy themselves with the Torah."

Although the center of the Jewish people and of Jewish learning was in Babylon at that time, the Land of Israel is mentioned first, out of respect and love for the Holy Land; and although only Babylon is mentioned with it, it includes all the lands of the exile, wherever Jews lived.

Interestingly, the length of the day and the year is fixed. There are no more than 24 hours in the day, and the years are of the same duration for all. So what is the meaning of "increased" days and "lengthened" years? In a deeper sense, the real length of time is determined by what one puts into it. The person who uses only half his time to good advantage, and wastes the rest, has only "half" a day; his days and years are "short." We pray for long days and long years – days and years filled to capacity with the things that are everlasting, the Torah and Mitzvot and good deeds.

There is also a second *Yekum Purkan*, immediately following the first. It is almost identical, except that the prayer is for the congregation.

May he who... מִי שֶׁעָשָׂה נִסִּים...

Recited standing, only on the Shabbat proceeding a new month.

On the Shabbat before Rosh Chodesh (New Moon), a special prayer for the new month is recited after the reading of the weekly portion of the Torah.

The central point of this custom is to announce the day (or two days) of the week on which Rosh Chodesh will occur. The custom of blessing the new month, with the announcement of the *molad* (time of apperance of the new moon) preceding it, reminds us of the symbolic link between the destiny of the Jewish people with the moon.

The moon has its periods of increasing and diminishing brightness. But even when it seems to be hidden in total darkness, it

126

is certain to "renew" itself and grow brighter until it attains its fullness. So too with our people throughout our long history; we rose from the darkness of Egyptian bondage to the heights of freedom as a "kingdom of *Kohanim* (God's servants) and a Holy Nation. We received the Torah at Mount Sinai, entered the Holy Land, built the Holy Temple, and were led by our kings and prophets. But it was never an even course.

There was the *churban* (destruction) and exile, followed by the return to the Land of Israel and the second Temple, with periods of eclipse under Greek oppression followed by regained freedom under the *chashmonaim*. But we soon fell under Roman occupation and the second churban, resulting in the exile and dispersion of our people to all the four corners of the earth in what is known as *Galut* Edom-our present, darkest but last exile.

And so Rosh Chodesh brings us a message of "renewal" and true consolation: no matter how dark it may be outside, there is no reason for despair, since this very month, perhaps even today, may bring the true and everlasting redemption.

♫ Transliteration:

Mi she-öso nisim la-avosaynu, v'gö-al osöm may-av'dus l'chay-rus, hu yig-al osönu b'körov, vi-kabaytz nidö-chaynu may-arba kan'fos hö-öretz, chavay-rim köl yisrö-ayl, v'nomar ömayn. **Wait for leader.**

Wait for the leader to recite and repeat after him: Rosh chodesh (name of month), ba-yom (day(s) of week), ha-bö ölaynu l'tovöh.

Continue with: Y'chad'shayhu ha-ködosh böruch hu ölaynu, v'al köl amo bays yisrö-ayl, l'cha-yim u-l'shölom, l'söson u-l'simchöh, l'shu-öh u-l'nechömöh, v'nomar ömayn.

Happy are those... אַשְׁרֵי יוֹשְׁבֵי...

This is the second time we recite this Psalm today. Here it serves as an opening to the additional Shabbat service called *Musaf*.

Our daily prayers, as well as our Shabbat, Rosh Chodesh, and Festival prayers correspond to the offerings in the Holy Temple of old. Since on Shabbat, Rosh Chodesh, and the Festivals there were additional offerings (*musafim*), we have on these festive days a special "additional" *Amidah*, called *Musaf*.

This service begins with a silent *Amidah*, followed with a repetition of the *Amidah* by the leader, and the concluding prayers.

Let them praise... יְהַלְלוּ...

Recited standing

As the Torah is returned to the ark we recite this passage.

Transliteration:

Y'hal'lu es shaym adonöy, ki nisgöv sh'mo l'vado. Hodo al eretz v'shömöyim. Va-yörem keren l'amo, t'hilöh l'chöl chasidöv, liv'nay yisrö-ayl am k'rovo ah-l'lu-yöh.

The Musaf Amidah

Blessed are You...   בָּרוּךְ אַתָּה...

The Amidah. Recited standing with feet together

We rise for the Amidah, the prayer in which we put forth our personal requests to God. (On Festivals, a special Amidah is substituted.) We take three steps back, and then three steps forward, as if approaching a king. At the word *Boruch*, blessed, we bend the knee; *Atoh*, You, we bow forward; and at *Adonoy*, Lord, we straighten up.

The benedictions of the Amidah are as old as our people, and date back to the times of Abraham, Isaac and Jacob, although the final form of it, as we know it in our Prayer books, dates back to a later time, to the time of Ezra the Scribe and the Men of the Great Assembly more than 2,300 years ago. That was the time of the Babylonian Exile, when the Jews were driven from their land into Babylon. Many began to forget the Hebrew language. It was then that

129

the leaders and prophets of Israel at that time – the Men of the Great Assembly – arranged the prayers in its fixed order, in Hebrew.

Thus all the Jews, at all times and in all places would be reciting the same holy prayers, in the same language, and this would give them a feeling of unity and strength.

This prayer is also known as the *Shemone Esrei*, which means "eighteen," because originally this prayer had eighteen blessings (weekday version). These blessings and passages are more than a collection of petitions or requests for ourselves, and our people. They also remind us of certain events in our history. According to our Sages, each blessing of the Shemone Esrei tells a story of some miracle that happened in the past, which was the first occasion when the blessing was said by the angels.

You have establised...   ...תִּקַּנְתָּ שַׁבָּת

This is the first prayer added to the Shabbat Musaf Amidah. If the shabbat occurs on Rosh Chodesh, we skip this prayer and resume with the regular prayers.

This prayer is composed in reverse alphabetical order, beginning with the last letter of the alephbet – Tav – and ending with the first letter – Aleph.

The alphabetical order is more than just a cute poetic form; it has special significance. Our Sages observe that it reflects and encompasses the totality of all the 22 holy letters of our Holy Tongue in which God's Torah has been written and given to us. Moreover, there is a significance also in whether the order is from *aleph* to *tav*, or in reverse, from *tav* to *aleph*. In general, the first symbolizes a movement from man to God; the second from God to man. Though both are integral parts in our mutual relationship with God, there are times when the initiative should come "from below," that is, from the individual, in terms of repentance and good deeds; other initiatives comes "from above," as an act of pure Divine grace and kindness, in order to trigger a corresponding response on the part of the favored individual.

In light of the above, it can be seen why the reverse order is the more appropriate one for this prayer of the Musaf Amidah, since the gift of Shabbat is an act of Divine grace, the culmination of the whole creation order, which was "created through kindness."

This prayer expresses our gratitude to God for having instituted the Shabbat, for taking pleasure in the special Shabbat service and also for making the Shabbat a unique source of blessing, so that those who delight in it inherit everlasting honor; those who taste it merit eternal life; those who love its precepts choose greatness.

The second part of this prayer expresses our fervent prayer that God should bring us up in joy to our land and plant us within its borders so that we can resume the Divine service in a restored *Beit Hamikdash*, with the daily and additional *musaf* offerings as prescribed for us in the Torah.

On the Shabbat...   ‫וּבְיוֹם הַשַּׁבָּת...‬

Here we quote the text in the Torah that describes the Musaf offering. This is explained by means of a parable: A king treated his servants to his royal table and served them two dishes. When he was ready for his own meal, the servants asked him, "What shall we serve you, our lord?" The king replied, "What is good for you is also good enough for me – just two lambs and two tenths of fine flour."

The intent of the sacrifices is that we are to realize that earthly food and produce are not an end to themselves, but they are to be utilized for a higher spiritual purpose. We are to use the energy and other derivatives from them to better serve God and follow His commandments.

Those who observe...   ‫יִשְׂמְחוּ...‬

The wording of this prayer, as in all prayers, is carefully chosen and meaningful.

Rejoicing is usually associated with our Festivals, but it also applies to Shabbat. Observing the Shabbat and keeping it holy brings us the sure promise of being satiated – gratified to the point of rejoicing – with God's goodness, both in this world and in the World To Come.

God called the Seventh Day "Desirable of Days." This means that while the Six Days of Creation were necessary to create the world, it is the Seventh Day that God really desired and made holy. In our life, too, living as we are in a material world, we are expected to work and toil during the six days of the week, but these days are not an end in themselves: they are but a means to attain a higher form of living, to rise to a state of holiness, which is personified by the Shabbat.

Our God...   אֱלֹהֵינוּ...

Examining the text of this prayer, we can see that it refers to both the "passive" and "active" aspects of Shabbat. As a day of rest from all work, we observe it simply by not doing any of the forbidden 39 kinds of work and their offshoots. This is the so-called "passive" aspect of Shabbat, and is referred to in this prayer by the words "accept with favor our (Shabbat) rest." At the same time, Shabbat has its "active" aspect, in that it is dedicated to Mitzvot and the study of Torah.

This is why the prayer continues with the words "sanctify us with Your commandments and grant us a portion in Your Torah." This refers to the fact that every Jew has a portion and share in the Torah. It may be impossible for every person to study and master the whole Torah, but no matter on what the level of understanding, one has a portion in the Torah. By studying Torah every day to the best of one's ability, one takes possession of one's very own 'share' in the Torah.

Look with Favor...   רְצֵה יְיָ...

This prayer begins the closing section of the Amidah. At *Modim*, 'We thankfully Acknowledge...' we gently bow with the first words of this prayer.

The Amidah is concluded by taking three steps back, as if departing from the presence of a king, at the verse *Oseh Sholom*, He who makes the peace, and three steps forward to complete the *Amidah*.

The Leader's Repetition of the Amidah

A repetition of the Amidah is recited by the leader. This custom was set in place around the time of the formulation of the Amidah. The leader repeated the Amidah for those who could not read the Hebrew, having them in mind.

The Kedusha

Recited standing, with our feet together

This is a special sanctification prayer recited in unison during the repitition of the Amidah. The congregation recites one verse at a time, followed by the leader.

There is a great deal of preparation going on among the angelic hosts before they utter their prayers to sanctify their Creator: *Kadosh, kadosh, kadosh* (Holy, holy, holy).

Kadosh also means "separate"; to say that "God is holy" is to say that God is separated from, and unaffected by, the world He created. The repetition of the word "holy" three times is explained in the Aramaic translation of the kedusha in the prayer of *U-va L'tzion*: "Holy in the heavens above, the abode of His glory; holy on earth, the work of His might; holy forever and ever."

While reciting this prayer, stand with your feet together and refrain from any interruption.

Transliteration:

Keser yit'nu l'chö adonöy elohaynu mal-öchim ha-monay ma-löh v'am'chö yisrö-ayl k'vutzay matöh yachad kulöm k'dushöh l'chö y'sha-layshu ka-kösuv al yad n'vi-echö v'körö zeh el zeh v'ömar. Wait for leader.

Ködosh, ködosh, ködosh, adonöy tz'vö-os m'lo chöl hö-öretz k'vodo. K'vodo mölay olöm m'shör-söv sho-alim zeh lözeh a-yay m'kom k'vodo l'ha-aritzo l'umösöm m'shab'chim v'om'rim. Wait for leader.

Böruch k'vod adonöy mim'komo. Mim'komo hu yifen b'rachamöv l'amo ha-m'yachadim sh'mo erev vövoker b'chöl yom tömid pa-ama-yim b'ahavöh sh'ma om'rim. Wait for leader.

Sh'ma yisrö-ayl, adonöy elohaynu, adonöy echöd. Hu elohaynu, hu övinu hu malkaynu hu moshi-aynu hu yoshi-aynu v'yig-ölaynu shaynis b'körov v'yashmi-aynu b'rachamöv l'aynay köl chai lay-mor hayn gö-alti es'chem a-charis kiv'rayshis lih-yos löchem lay-lohim. Wait for leader.

Ani adonöy elo-haychem.Wait for leader.

Yimloch adonöy l'olöm eloha-yich tziyon l'dor vödor, hal'lu-yöh. Wait for leader. You may be seated when the leader concludeds the blessing.

The Modim

Recited standing, while the leader recites *Modim*.

ꋬ **Transliteration:**

Modim anach-nu löch, shö-atöh hu adonöy elo-haynu vay-lohay avosaynu elohay köl bösör, yotz'raynu, yotzayr b'rayshis. B'röchos v'hodö-os l'shim'chö hagödol v'haködosh, al she-heche-yisönu v'kiyam-tönu. kayn t'cha-yaynu us'ka-y'maynu v'se-esof gölu-yosay-nu l'chatzros ködshechö, v'nösuv ay-lechö lishmor chukechö, v'la-asos r'tzonechö, ul'övd'chö b'layvöv shölaym, al she-önu modim löch. Böruch ayl ha-hodö-os.

There is none...   ...אֵין כֵּאלֹהֵינוּ

After the conclusion of the repetition of the *Amidah* the leader recites whole kaddish and we continue with this prayer. This prayer begins the concluding prayers of the morning service.

After trekking through the whole service we proudly and earnestly give voice to the deep feelings of awe and gratitude we have for God. And this is expressed so profoundly in this five stanza hymn.

Notice how the first three stanzas of this prayer from the acrostic of Amen.

Transliteration:

Ayn kaylo-haynu, ayn kado-naynu, ayn k'malkaynu, ayn k'moshi-aynu.

Mi chaylo-haynu, mi chado-naynu, mi ch'malkaynu, mi ch'moshi-aynu.

Nodeh laylo-haynu, nodeh lado-naynu, nodeh l'malkaynu, nodeh l'moshi-aynu.

Böruch elo-haynu, böruch adonaynu, böruch malkaynu, böruch moshi-aynu.

Atöh hu elohaynu, atöh hu ado-naynu, atöh hu malkaynu, atöh hu moshi-aynu, atöh soshi-aynu.

Atöh sökum t'rachaym tzi-yon ki ays l'chen'nöh ki vö mo-ayd. Atöh hu adonöy elohaynu vay-lohay avo-saynu, she-hiktiru avosaynu l'fönechö es k'tores ha-samim.

The incense...   ...פִּטוּם הַקְּטֹרֶת

This is a Talmudic section on the composition of the incense which used to be offered in the Holy Temple twice daily, morning and evening.

The rising smoke of the *ketoret* (incense) symbolized our soul's yearning to soar heavenward, a yearning that could be fulfilled only through the fulfillment of the Divine commandments.

The Midrash states that the Hebrew word *ketoret* forms an acrostic of the initial letters of the four Hebrew words:

K—kedusha (holiness).

T—Tahara (purity).

R—Rachamim (mercy).

T—Tikvah (hope).

We find in the *Zohar* many passages on the importance of the daily recital of the ketoret (recited instead of offered since the Holy

138

Temple no longer stands in Jerusalem). One passage reads: The person who recites the portion of ketoret with devotion every day, will be spared any manner of sorrow or hurt all that day.

Kaddish D'rabonon

Recited standing

This is a special prayer for the Rabbis, scholars and students of the Torah. It is recited by a mourner at the conclusion of the services.

Ᵽ **Transliteraion:**

Yis-gadal v'yis-kadash sh'may raböh.

(Cong: Ömayn)

B'öl'mö di v'rö chir'u-say v'yamlich mal'chusay, v'yatzmach pur'könay viköräyv m'shi-chay.

(Cong: Ömayn)

B'cha-yay-chon u-v'yomaychon u-v'cha-yay d'chöl bays yisro-ayl, ba-agölö u-viz'man köriv v'im'ru ömayn.

(Cong: Ömayn. Y'hay sh'mayh rabö m'vörach l'ölam u-l'öl'may öl'ma-yö, yisböraych.)

Y'hay sh'mayh rabö m'vörach l'ölam u-l'öl'may öl'ma-yö. Yisböraych, v'yishtabach, v'yispö-ayr, v'yisromöm, v'yis-nasay, v'yis-hadör, v'yis-aleh, v'yis-halöl, sh'may d'kudshö b'rich hu.

(Cong: Ömayn)

L'aylö min köl bir'chösö v'shirösö, tush-b'chösö v'neche-mösö, da-amirön b'öl'mö, v'im'ru ömayn.

(Cong: Ömayn)

Al yisrö-ayl v'al rabönön, v'al tal-midayhon, v'al köl tal-miday sal-midayhon, v'al köl mön d'ös'kin b'oray'sö. Di v'asrö hödayn, v'di v'chlö asar v'asar. Y'hay l'hon u-l'chon shlömö rabö, chinö v'chisdö v'rachamin v'cha-yin arichin, u-m'zonö r'vichö u-fur'könö min ködöm avu-hon div'sh'ma-yö v'im'ru ömayn.

(Cong: Ömayn)

Y'hay sh'lömö rabö min sh'ma-yö, v'cha-yim tovim ölaynu v'al köl yisrö-ayl v'im'ru ömayn.

(Cong: Ömayn)

Take three steps back: Oseh shölom (Between Rosh HaShonoh and Yom Kippur substitute: ha-shölom) bim'romöv, hu ya-aseh shölom ölaynu v'al köl yisrö-ayl, v'im'ru ömayn. Take three steps forward.

(Cong: Ömayn)

It is incumbent...   עָלֵינוּ...

Recited standing

Our Sages tell us this prayer was composed by Joshua, as he led the children of Israel into the Promised Land. And if you look carefully you will find that the initials taken from the first letter of each sentence in the first paragraph, read backwards, form his name "Hoshua."

Thus, when Joshua was about to settle the Jewish people in the Holy Land, he made them remember, through this hymn, that they were different from the Canaanite peoples and other nations and tribes of the earth, who "worship vain things and emptiness."

Transliteration:

Ölaynu l'shabay-ach la-adon hakol, lösays g'dulöh l'yotzayr b'rayshis, shelo ösönu k'go-yay hö-arötzos, v'lo sömönu k'mish-p'chos hö-adömöh, shelo söm chelkaynu köhem, v'gorölaynu k'chöl ha-monöm sehaym mishtachavim l'hevel v'lörik. Va-anachnu kor'im u-mishtachavim u-modim, lif'nay melech, mal'chay ha-m'löchim, ha-ködosh böruch hu. She-hu noteh shöma-yim v'yosayd öretz, u-moshav y'köro ba-shöma-yim mima-al, u-sh'chinas u-zo b'göv'hay m'romim, hu elohaynu ayn od. Emes malkaynu, efes zulöso, kakösuv b'soröso. V'yöda-tö ha-yom vaha-shayvosö el l'vövechö, ki adonöy hu hö-elohim ba-shöma-yim mima-al, v'al hö-öretz mi-töchas, ayn od.

V'al kayn n'kaveh l'chö adonöy elohaynu lir-os m'hayröh b'sif-eres u-zechö, l'ha-avir gilulim min hö-öretz v'hö-elilim köros yiköray-sun, l'sakayn olöm b'mal'chus shadai, v'chöl b'nay vösör yik-r'u vish'mechö, l'hafnos ay-lechö köl rish-ay öretz. Yakiru v'yayd'u köl yosh'vay sayvayl, ki l'chö tichra köl berech, tishöva köl löshon. L'fönechö adonöy elohaynu yich-r'u v'yipolu, v'lich'vod shim'chö y'kör yitaynu vi-kab'lu chulöm alayhem es ol mal'chusechö, v'simloch alayhem m'hayröh l'olöm vö-ed, ki ha-mal'chus shel'chö hi, u-l'ol'may ad timloch b'chövod, ka-kösuv b'sorösechö, adonöy yimloch l'olöm vö-ed. V'ne-emar, v'hö-yöh adonöy l'melech al köl hö-öretz, ba-yom hahu yih-yeh adonöy echöd u-sh'mo echöd.

Mourner's Kaddish

Recited standing

At the conclusion of *Olaynu*, when praying with a quorum of at least ten Jewish male adults, mourners recite this Kaddish.

🎵 **Transliteration:**

Yis-gadal v'yis-kadash sh'may raböh.

(Cong: Ömayn)

B'öl'mö di v'rö chir'u-say v'yamlich mal'chusay, v'yatzmach pur'könay viköraym m'shi-chay.

(Cong: Ömayn)

B'cha-yay-chon u-v'yomaychon u-v'cha-yay d'chöl bays yisro-ayl, ba-agölö u-viz'man köriv v'im'ru ömayn.

(Cong: Ömayn. Y'hay sh'mayh rabö m'vörach l'ölam u-l'öl'may öl'ma-yö, yisböraych.)

Y'hay sh'mayh rabö m'vörach l'ölam u-l'öl'may öl'ma-yö. Yisböraych, v'yishtabach, v'yispö-ayr, v'yisromöm, v'yis-nasay, v'yis-hadör, v'yis-aleh, v'yis-halöl, sh'may d'kudshö b'rich hu.

(Cong: Ömayn)

L'aylö min köl bir'chösö v'shirösö, tush-b'chösö v'neche-mösö, da-amirön b'öl'mö, v'im'ru ömayn.

(Cong: Ömayn)

Y'hay sh'lömö rabö min sh'ma-yö, v'cha-yim tovim ölaynu v'al köl yisrö-ayl v'im'ru ömayn.

(Cong: Ömayn)

Take three steps back: Oseh shölom (Between Rosh HaShonoh and Yom Kippur substitute: ha-shölom) bim'romöv, hu ya-aseh shölom ölaynu v'al köl yisrö-ayl, v'im'ru ömayn. Take three steps forward.

(Cong: Ömayn)

Do not fear...   אַל תִּירָא...

Recited standing

These meaningful verses express an important message to us as we conclude the service and are about to part ways.

They remind us that no matter how long our exile may be, or what fears and anxieties beset us, God will always 'carry' us. We are God's 'burden' and responsibility, and God will never drop this burden. He will surely deliver us from our enemies and from the exile.

🏳 **Transliteration:**

Al tirö mipachad pis-om, u-misho-as r'shö-im ki sövo. U-tzu aytzöh v'suför, dab'ru dövör v'lo yökum, ki imönu ayl. V'ad zik-nöh ani hu, v'ad sayvöh ani esbol, ani ösisi va-ani esö, va-ani esbol va-amalayt. Ach tzadikim yodu lish'mechö yay-sh'vu y'shörim es pö-nechö.

At this point it is customary to recite Psalms as it has been divided for each day of the month. These are usually marked in the Book of Psalms.

Kaddish D'rabonon

Recited standing

This is a special prayer for the Rabbis, scholars and students of the Torah. It is recited by a mourner at the conclusion of the services.

🏳 **Transliteraion:**

Yis-gadal v'yis-kadash sh'may raböh.

(Cong: Ömayn)

B'öl'mö di v'rö chir'u-say v'yamlich mal'chusay, v'yatzmach pur'könay viköroyv m'shi-chay.

(Cong: Ömayn)

B'cha-yay-chon u-v'yomaychon u-v'cha-yay d'chöl bays yisro-ayl, ba-agölö u-viz'man köriv v'im'ru ömayn.

(Cong: Ömayn. Y'hay sh'mayh rabö m'vörach l'ölam u-l'öl'may öl'ma-yö, yisböraych.)

144

Y'hay sh'mayh rabö m'vörach l'ölam u-l'öl'may öl'ma-yö. Yisböraych, v'yishtabach, v'yispö-ayr, v'yisromöm, v'yis-nasay, v'yis-hadör, v'yis-aleh, v'yis-halöl, sh'may d'kudshö b'rich hu.

(Cong: Ömayn)

L'aylö min köl bir'chösö v'shirösö, tush-b'chösö v'neche-mösö, da-amirön b'öl'mö, v'im'ru ömayn.

(Cong: Ömayn)

Al yisrö-ayl v'al rabönön, v'al tal-midayhon, v'al köl tal-miday sal-midayhon, v'al köl mön d'ös'kin b'oray'sö. Di v'asrö hödayn, v'di v'chlö asar v'asar. Y'hay l'hon u-l'chon shlömö rabö, chinö v'chisdö v'rachamin v'cha-yin arichin, u-m'zonö r'vichö u-fur'könö min ködöm avu-hon div'sh'ma-yö v'im'ru ömayn.

(Cong: Ömayn)

Y'hay sh'lömö rabö min sh'ma-yö, v'cha-yim tovim ölaynu v'al köl yisrö-ayl v'im'ru ömayn.

(Cong: Ömayn)

Take three steps back: Oseh shölom (Between Rosh HaShonoh and Yom Kippur substitute: ha-shölom) bim'romöv, hu ya-aseh shölom ölaynu v'al köl yisrö-ayl, v'im'ru ömayn. Take three steps forward.

(Cong: Ömayn)

-This concludes the morning services-

"The power of the prayer of a simple Jew"

- A Story -

It was Yom Kippur Eve. A breathless hush took hold of the congregation as all eyes turned upon the figure of their revered Ba'al Shem Tov. He stood there, dressed in his white *kittel* (special garment worn on Yom Kippur) and wrapped in his *Tallit* which covered also his bent head. As everyone waited whilst the Ba'al Shem Tov prepared himself for the sacred prayer of "*Kol Nidrei*," those nearer to him saw a shadow pass over his face, but no one dared ask him what was wrong.

His obvious distress was reflected in the faces of all present, as they recited the very moving *Kol Nidrei* prayer. During the brief pause between *Kol Nidrei* and the evening service, the Ba'al Shem Tov again became sunk in thought. Suddenly, a gentle smile lit up his face and, as he asked that the services begin. Everyone present felt a relief which they did not understand. They did not know the reason for their beloved Rabbi's earlier distress, nor did they know the reason why he smiled. All they knew was that whatever affected their saintly leader, also deeply affected each and every one of them.

At the conclusion of Yom Kippur, the Ba'al Shem Tov told his followers the following story:

"My friends," he said, "I am going to tell you what affected me so deeply last night during the davening. The story is connected with a Jewish innkeeper in a nearby village. The innkeeper was a very fine, honest and observant Jew, whom the landlord, a Polish nobleman, greatly admired and treated as a personal friend. Suddenly, without any warning illness, the innkeeper died, leaving behind him a young widow with a baby boy. The poor young woman became deeply affected by her loss, and before long, she, too died.

"The Polish nobleman was very upset about the passing of his tenant and friend, and when the widow also died, he felt it was his duty to take the baby into his care now that it was a helpless orphan. He was a very kind man and gave the baby the best care and brought him up as his own son.

"Years passed and the child did not know that he was not, in truth, the real son of the Christian nobleman. One day, however, the nobleman had invited some friends of his to visit him at his estate, and whilst their children were playing together in the garden, one of them in the course of a quarrel called the nobleman's 'son' a Jew. The boy quickly ran up to the nobleman crying, and asked him if it was really true that he is a Jew?

"'My dear boy,' he replied gently. 'You know how much I love you and that I have treated you as if you were my very own son. When I die you will be my heir; I'll leave everything to you — my estate, my orchards and my forests. What more could I do for you?'

"'So I'm not your real son! So I am a Jew and you never told me,' the boy burst out sobbing. 'Who were my parents? I have to know, please!'

"The nobleman put his arms around the boy's shoulders, trying to comfort him. 'My boy, you can be proud of your parents. They were very fine people indeed; good, God-fearing Jews. Your father was my friend. It was for his sake that I felt it was my duty to take you into my home and bring you up as I would my own son. But you know I have no other children and I love you very dearly.'

"Bit by bit the boy got the whole story of his own Jewish parents. The nobleman told him that his parents had nothing at all to leave him excepting a small package which he had hidden away in a safe place, waiting for the right moment to give it to him.

The moment had now come and so he went and brought the package and gave it to the boy. With trembling hands and a quickly beating heart the boy opened the package and beheld an old black velvet bag with strange gold lettering on it. He opened the bag and took out a white wool shawl, something else which looked like two small black boxes wound around with black leather straps, and a book. Of course the boy did not know what the *Tallit* (prayer shawl) and *Tefillin* (phylacteries) were, nor could he understand what was in the thick book, which was a Siddur. But because these precious things had once belonged to his parents, his real parents, whom he had never known, he meant to treasure them as long as he lived!

"By a lucky chance, the nobleman had to leave on a business trip, which gave the boy a chance to think in peace and quiet. He took long walks in the woods and spent hours thinking. He realized that he loved the nobleman and was grateful to him, and yet — a strange feeling took hold of him which urged him to seek out his Jewish brethren. He knew there were some who lived on his 'father's' estates. He would go and see them; talk to them. Perhaps some of them even remembered his parents!

"That night he dreamt that his parents came to him, first his father, then his mother. They told him he was now no more a child. He must know he is a Jew and go back to his Jewish people where he belongs.

"The next day, very early, he quickly crept out of the house so that none of the servants should stop him or question him. He walked until he reached the next village where he saw some Jews packing some bundles on to carts.

"'Good day to you,' he called to them. 'Are you going to a fair?'

"'No, not this time,' they replied. 'It will soon be our holy Festival, Yom Kippur, so we are taking our families to the next big town, so that at least at this sacred time we can all pray in the synagogue with other Jews.'

"The boy returned home lost in thought. Why had he not taken his parents' gift with him to show to these Jews? They would have told him what they were for. The thought gave him no rest. Also, what was Yom Kippur?

"A few days went by and the nobleman had not yet returned. The boy suddenly decided he was old enough to make up his own mind about this thing which affected his very future. He was a Jew and he meant to go back to his people! So he packed a few clothes together, took some food along, left a note telling his 'father' where he had gone, and set off for the town to which the village Jews had said they were going.

"After several weary days of traveling, getting a 'hitch' when he could, but mostly walking, he finally reached his destination. He found out where the shul was and reached it just as the haunting notes of the Kol Nidrei service were being sung. Quietly, the boy slipped inside and took a place near the door. The scene which met his gaze filled him with awe. He looked around him and beheld Jews of all ages praying with all their hearts, some with tears in their eyes. He felt a lump come into his own throat as he quietly took out his own white shawl and wrapped it around his shoulders.

He took out his book and tried to hold it as he saw the others holding theirs. But when he opened it and could neither read nor understand the words, sobs suddenly shook his young body.

"With the tears streaming down his cheeks, the lad cried out: 'O, God! You know I cannot read, nor do I know what to say and how to pray. I am just a lost Jewish boy! Here is the whole prayer book! Please, dear God, take out the right words to form the prayers for me!'

"The despair of this poor Jewish lad reached the Heavenly Court on High, and the gates were flung open for his prayer. And together with his simple prayer, our prayers, too, were accepted."

When the Ba'al Shem Tov finished this moving story, tears stood in the eyes of all his listeners. And often, when praying, they thought about this strange story of the young Jewish lad who had been lost for a time. And they thought of themselves that they, too, were often like lost souls who did not really know how to pray as well as they should. They all earnestly hoped, like the boy, that the kind and merciful God on High would accept their prayers, and grant each and all a truly happy New Year, for the important thing about prayer is, after all, the sincerity and devotion to God, which come from the heart.

"Of Kings and Souls"
- A Parable -

A princess, an only child, was very beloved and spoiled by her father, the King. Artists and musicians came daily to entertain her. Designers created her exquisite clothing. The finest chefs prepared her meals, and her friends were only people of culture and class.

When she was of marriageable age, she could find no match. No prince suited her fancy, no noble was good enough for her, no socialite was charming or dashing enough. The king became so annoyed that he decreed: "The very next suitor to walk in will be your husband!"

Moments later, a young gardener who had lost his way in the palace appeared. The horrified princess looked at the gardener. He, for his part, tried to hastily retreat, apologizing all the while. But the king was a man of his word. The princess would wed this common gardener!

When the princess got to know her husband, she found him to be kind and gentle, albeit simple. She began to enjoy her unrestricted lifestyle: she did what she wanted, wore what she chose, ate what she pleased. It was exhilarating to be "free."

Months passed thus, and then one day, the gardener returned home to find a forlorn wife. He pondered the situation and then had an idea.

"I have guessed the cause of your despondency," he announced. "Weeks have passed since we've had tomatoes, as the tomato season is over. You must miss them. I will find tomatoes, and though they may be very expensive, what importance is money unless it can be used to make you happy?" The gardener looked at his wife and to his surprise saw large tears rolling down her cheeks.

The following evening, the gardener came home with a gift. "My dearest, yesterday I erred. I realize that in the palace, you did not work. Now you are doing jobs that must be hard for you. The broom handle, which is rough and unpolished, must surely hurt your tender hands. I have brought you a broom with a smooth handle!" The princess burst into bitter tears, and buried her head.

Every Jew has a soul which, until it descends into this world, resides at the foot of the Throne of Glory, delighting in God's presence and enjoying a close relationship with God. This is because the soul is truly the King's daughter. Eventually the soul must come into this world to accomplish a mission. The soul is wed to the "gardener" – the body. She becomes enamored by her apparent freedom and by the delights and novelties which did not exist in the King's palace.

But one day, the soul feels a strange longing. She can do what she pleases and the gardener is indeed pleasant. But, she misses the King's palace. "I did not appreciate what I had, and even felt restricted. But now I understand that those were special rights and privileges."

The gardener – the body – sensing that his wife is unhappy, tries to find a solution. But his simple intellect can conceive of nothing more than tomatoes and broom sticks. He offers his wife these crude objects in the hope that they will satisfy her. "We'll buy a leather sofa and loveseat, and a projection TV. We'll move to a new house in a nicer neighborhood, with pickled-wood floors." But the soul can no longer restrain herself. "Everything is really wonderful and pleasant, but this is not the problem. I yearn for the life of royalty and how can you, a simple and coarse body, comprehend me? You understand furniture and food, but do you know what closeness to God is? About Torah and mitzvot? These are things which will always be foreign to you, and therefore you cannot understand why I am sad, and what I am really lacking!"

Especially during prayer, our souls cry out to us to be heard and understood. "Do not try to placate me with tomatoes or even sun-dried tomatoes, with smooth broom handles or a central vacuum system. I am the King's daughter; help me renew and enhance my connection to my Father in

Heaven." This is accomplished through the words of prayer and the performance of mitzvot.

-*Quick How-To Guides*-

Pesicha - Opening the Ark

1) Rise and proceed to the ark. Once there, stand facing the ark.

2) When indicated, open the curtain (and doors) and remain standing.

3) When the congregation has completed the special prayer, remove the Torah (the *Gabbai* will usually indicate which one), hold it upright with both hands, and lean it on your right shoulder.

4) Bring and give the Torah to the *Chazzan*, prayer leader, and return to your seat.

Aliyah - Going up for a Torah portion

1) Rise and proceed to the reading table where to Torah is being read.

2) Approach the Torah on the right side of the reader. The Torah will be opened and the portion that will be read will be indicated to you. Take the *Gartel* (Torah belt) and touch the scroll at the beginning and end of where it will be read, then kiss the *Gartel*.

3) Put the *Gartel* down and roll the Torah closed. Recite aloud the blessing while holding the two Torah handles, one in each hand. Allow time for the congregation to answer *Amen*, after each blessing.

4) After the blessing, the Torah will be opened. Remain standing in position while the reader reads the portion. During this time hold the right Torah handle with your right hand and try to follow along silently.

5) At the conclusion of the reading, take the *Gartel* and touch the end and beginning of the portion just read. Kiss the *Gartel*, put it down, and roll the Torah closed.

6) Recite aloud the final blessing, while holding the Torah handles with both of your hands. When you have concluded the blessing, move to the right side of the reading table and remain standing there until the next person has completed his portion and blessings. He will then take your place at the side of the reading table, and you should return to your seat.

Haggbah - Lifting the Torah

1) Rise and proceed to the reading table where to Torah is being read.

2) Stand in front of the Torah, and when indicated, roll open the Torah to a span of at least three columns. Take the *Gartel* (Torah belt) and pass it over the Torah portions, touching the Torah. Kiss the *Gartel* and put it down.

3) Hold both Torah handles, and bring the Torah forward, bringing the handles just off the table.

4) Bear down, and with one motion, lift the Torah upright, keeping it spread open. Turn right, then left, displaying the scroll to the congregation.

5) Place the Torah back on the reading table, and roll it closed. Lift it up and sit down behind you. Another person will dress the Torah with its garments.

6) Remain sitting until indicated to return the Torah to the Ark. Once there, give the Torah to the person standing there, and he will place it in the Ark. You may now return to your seat.

Gelilah - Dressing the Torah

1) Rise and proceed to the reading table where to Torah is being held.

2) Make sure the Torah is rolled closed, with a column seam at the center.

3) Take the belt and secure it around the Torah. It should rest on the lower third.

4) Put the mantel on the Torah, with the front facing away from you, followed by the other ornaments.

5) Return to your seat.

-*Synagogue Glossary*-

Aliyah: Being called up to the Torah.
Amen (lit., "true"): Acknowledgement.
Amidah (lit., "standing"): Silent Prayer.
Amud (lit., "stand"): Prayer stand.
Aron Kodesh (lit., "holy ark"): Ark where the Torah is stored.
Becher (Yiddish): Cup used for Kiddush.
Besamim: Fragrant spices used for Havdalah.
Bimah (lit., "stage"): Reading Table.
Birkat Hagomel: Thanksgiving blessing.
Birkat Kohanim: Preistly Blessing.
Chazzan (lit., "cantor"): Prayer Leader.
Ezrat Noshim: Women Section.
Gabbai: Organizer; assistant.
Gartel (Yiddish): Tie for the Torah; special prayer belt.
Gellilah: Binding the Torah.
Genizah: Repository of worn Hebrew texts.
Haftorah: Portion from the Prophets.
Hagboh: Lifting the Torah.
Hallel (lit., "praise"): Read on Rosh Chodesh and Holidays.
Kaadish: Mourners Prayer.
Keter: Torah Crown.
Kiddush: Ceremonial procedure; celebratory luncheon.
Kiddush Hachodesh: Blessing the new month.

Kiddush Levanah: Blessing of the new moon.
Kippah: Head covering.
Kittle: Special garment worn on Yom Kippur.
Maariv: Evening Service.
Mechitza: Partition.
Mincha: Afternoon Service.
Minyan: Quorum of ten adult Jewish males.
Ner Tomid: Eternal Light.
Parasha: Portion.
Pirkay Avot: Reading from Ethics of our Fathers.
Poroches: Curtain covering the ark.
Seudat Mitzvah: Commemorative Meal.
Shacharit: Morning Service.
Shalosh Seudot: Third Shabbat meal.
Shtender: Prayer stand.
Shulchan: Reading table.
Siddur: Prayer Book.
Taalit: Prayer shawl.
Tehillim: Psalms, the book of.
Tetzel: Dish for the Kiddush cup.
Tzedakah: Charity.
Yad (lit., "hand"): Hand Pointer for the Torah.
Yarmulka: Head covering.

5 Books of Moses,
613 Commandments,
14 Million Jewish People,
1 Solution

THE JEWISH LEARNING GROUP
was created to produce innovative educational products
geared toward the beginner in Judaism.

THE JEWISH LEARNING GROUP
offers extensive how-to guides on Jewish law and custom, traditional
prayer texts with transliteration and instruction, and other innovative
audio and visual materials. Now, everyone can reap the rudimentary
knowledge and confidence necessary to lead and further his or her
Jewish observance at a comfortable and gradual pace.